Thoughts From A Friend

Thoughts From A Friend

Jami Lynch Rogers
and
Norm Sawyer

ISBN 10: 1-988226-59-7
ISBN 13: 978-1-988226-59-0

Cover Art: Kane Sawyer
Photos: Jami and Norm

Published by

First Page Solutions
Kelowna, BC, Canada

Dedication

To all of our friends.

Contents

Part One:

Love

Free

They chance as whispers
when the day is high,
drifting as one in the sapphire bliss-
caressing sunbeams with gentle feathers
Stolen moments in the endless mist.

To sigh their morning golden hues
breathe among the stars of night,
and rage as storms with peaceful vanishings,
to roll in rain, framed by its light

with a jealous huff of wind they part
ever-shifting, they divide,
swirling passion, ghostly fading-
They break so love can fly.

Jami

On the Trail To Love

Love one another
John 13:34

In my quest to love better, I have found myself among the lesser travelled, more challenging trails of my own heart. I am looking inward and around me, and observing love with its many peaks and valleys. It's easy to love people who love me back, and it's such a gift to have someone in my life who accepts me as my unique self, but also pushes me to my potential and holds me accountable. I don't trust lightly, so to find someone who stays consistently in my life, and doesn't leave when things get tough is pretty admirable to me. Even if a mistake is made between us, because there is security in the way we feel about each other and treat each other, it's natural to just talk it over and move on. I love and relax in those kinds of relationships and I want all of my relationships to have that kind of integrity, grace, and openness. I desire healthy, loving relationships in which we build each other up, call each other out, and grow in faith, together.

Why was it in certain relationships, I tried so hard and it was just fruitless and in others it was just so effortless? Was it me? Was it them? The biggest question is why was I having to try so hard? I gave so much, and expected either nothing or too much. I made excuses for the other person, ignoring toxic behavior. I had my eye on the potential of the relationship, but refused to see it for what it actually was or had become at that time. I pushed myself on the whole 'love one another' campaign to a fault, at my own expense, because I failed to put protective boundaries in place. I became the toxic person, in a sense. I wasn't being appreciated for who I was, and I wasn't being treated the way I wanted to be treated, and I made excuses for that too. Because love makes excuses, right? No, but not wanting to see the truth sure does.

I've since come to understand that just adding love and copious attention is too simple. I've invested in people that didn't end up staying in my life, and I've extended love and multiple chances, and lost sleep and tears to people who dropped me like yesterday's newspaper. I've loved people who hurt me over and over. Love one another, yes. Love even when it's difficult to do. Love people through all their hard times, ridiculous situations, and wart-filled moments, because I'm not perfect either, right? But love doesn't always mean sticking around for the shrapnel of others. **Make no friendship with a man given to anger, nor go with a wrathful man.** Proverbs 22:24 Love is not enough to make everything better, but it's still the right answer. **Bear with each other and forgive one another if any of you has a grievance against someone. Forgive as the Lord forgave you.** Colossians 3:13 As my dear and devoted friend Norm would tell me, "Miss Jami, stop watering dead plants." I finally honored myself and I did. I told myself the truth, and I tearfully moved on. That trail was a rough one to walk alone. Sometimes loving someone means distance and forgiveness and letting God lead the rest of the uncharted way. Loving yourself means putting up short fences in order to keep yourself from going down trails that continue to lead to heartache.

I think relationships can be challenging at times, but love is not. I've been told I have a huge, soft heart, and sometimes it gets me into trouble. I love hard, I give too much, I end up hurting a lot, and I feel depleted many times when what I want to give is rejected. This is why there are benches along the trail. I just need to sit with those feelings, because they are not to be acted upon. I realized through these failed relationships that I was struggling with feelings of abandonment and rejection, and it was a fear of facing those feelings that kept me watering these dead relationships.

God wants us to love one another, yes. We are His children, and we are to be loving and forgiving toward one another. But He doesn't want us to remain in toxic, damaging, or unhealthy relationships. If we find ourselves engaging in unhealthy interactions or behavior with anyone, and we are putting energy and effort into people that are leading us into sin, or even just not responding to that attention, it's time to create distance in those relationships, not just add more love. God often takes us out of relationships that we beg and fight for, because they are not up to His standards, and in my case, I was fighting against my feelings of being rejected and wanting someone else to validate that. Only God can heal that. **For**

where you have envy and selfish ambition, there you find disorder and every evil practice. James 3:16 Sometimes we need to sit with that pain and listen to what God wants us to do within that relationship instead of following our own wills and desires. One of the things that has given me peace and has helped me to maneuver my heart better through these hills and brambles I encounter, is the fact that it is God's love that I have to share, and not just my own. He has filled me with this love. If I put Him in charge of the love I give, I don't have to be hurt when it gets rejected anymore. **He heals the brokenhearted and binds up their wounds.** Psalm 147:3

Therefore, as God's chosen people, holy and dearly loved, clothe yourselves with compassion, kindness, humility, gentleness, and patience. Colossians 3:12

When we are full of love and compassion for others and ourselves, we become powerful. When we are powerful, we can choose to not allow the careless words and actions of others to get to our hearts so personally. We can understand that it's not always about us, though it's okay to have feelings and deal with them in a healthy way. It is with compassion that Jesus healed the people. **When Jesus landed and saw a large crowd, he had compassion on them and healed their sick.** Matthew 14:14 We can be helpful healers of people as well when we show compassion to them instead of anger or bitterness when they make mistakes or let us down. We can also help heal ourselves when we are tender toward ourselves and our own mistakes.

Genuine, authentic love involves desiring what is best for others-even people we don't like, people who walked away or hurt us, or people we see as our enemies, because when we are softened by the love and compassion that is God within us, we can let go of resentments and judgments and be open to forgiveness. This could be the longest, most arduous part of the trail as humans, but the most worthwhile. The time that we spend trying to understand how we can improve ourselves, where we need to accept correction, and how we can better pour honest love and forgiveness into the people that are placed in our paths.

I will continue on my trail to love, seeking to love the way in which God has created me; stepping gently, gracefully, and with a big, open heart.

Love is patient, love is kind. It does not envy, it does not boast, it is not proud. It does not dishonor others, it is not self-seeking, it is not easily angered, it keeps no record of wrongs. Love does not delight in evil but rejoices with the truth. It always protects, always trusts, always hopes, always perseveres. Love never fails.
1Corinthians 13:4-8

Jami

My Lady Arc

I see your frame in a shadowed silhouette.
Your strength, like Joan of Arc, is consumed with fire,
Helplessly surrounded by the touching of my hand.
You burn with the sound of my heart and breath.
I am the stake you are tied to with rings of gold.
The vow is the strength of the embrace we hold
Until our wishes are full and souls realized.
Now you are the candle's flame, a steady warmth and glow.
You light the path our love will take, as God ordained it so.

Norm

Antigua

I like to reach into the memory of my soul to relive the night my wife and I enjoyed the sweetest of Latin ambiance in the old city of Antigua in Guatemala.

We had enjoyed the tastiest of foods and the surrounding beauty of art-covered walls and 16th century Spanish ornaments and furnishings that generously gave the rooms a life of their own. The name of this gallant restaurant is called El Sereno.

We had been generous in our affections, one to another, and had allowed our carefree feelings to dictate and direct the moods of this enchanted evening. Afterwards, with great expression, we said goodnight and goodbyes to the waiters and proprietor 'Pablo'. We found ourselves outside the frontage of this 'ambient colonial' restaurant leaning on each other, the way lovers do when first learning to express affection one to another.

I was totally lost in the rapture of that moment when a warm velvet breeze caressed both of us with clear insight into our love. As

I looked down the street, I could see the soft glow of lights that came from the different cafes along the cobblestone street and the ornamental iron workings that encased window ledges that supported reams of crimson red geraniums and splashes of multi-colored impatiens.

The fragrance of flowers in the night, coffee, and old stone ruins were blending a perfume made only for my wife and I to not forget our vows to each other. Yes, I'm convinced that is what the aromatic elixir was saying to me.

We listened to the hypnotic sounds of soft voices and lofty music that moved in the air with the beat that is truly characteristic to Central America. It is a rhythm and sound that enters your veins and becomes engrafted into your very being.

It was like we had stepped back one hundred, maybe two hundred years, and touched the lovers of old who had walked the same stone covered streets years ago. They were telling us that what we had was good, and the love we felt was ours to be enjoyed with the enthusiasm of the newly-wedded.

This talisman was given to us in November of 1992, and to this day I can still feel and experience the wooing of that night. I keep its friendship close to my heart where my rib and soul can visit and partake of this memory of love.

Norm

The Heart Is Real

A heart is weakness, it is strength
A peaceful union of give and take
A war of trusting and concealing
To hold or to forsake.
It wonders and it wanders
With its gentleness and fury,
It is timid, it is certain,
It is judge and it is jury.
It is steady, it is trembling
Wears conviction like a shield,
Yet fear can send it reeling
Baring open wounds unhealed.
A heart is tender, holding on
Tender, letting go
Broken, restored by love itself,
Broken by love gone cold.
The heart is fickle, it is constant
It fails, it never fails.
It is a balm, it is an ache
It smiles, it rejoices, it wails.
Our hearts are buried deep inside,
But in our eyes revealed

They beat in time with those who see
The love we can't conceal.
It is human, it is God.
Love is real.

Jami

Monterico's Lilies

Satin white water lilies, anchored by their flush green tubular root stems, bobbed on the water's surface. Brightly floral heads were shimmering and reflecting their calm as we floated by on the waterways that interlocked the land to the mangroves and the mangroves to the coastal ocean shore.

Prodding its way through the dark green waters, the twenty-five foot flatbed boat with a shabby lean-to roof and small outboard motor seemed to know its way through the thick and rich maze of mangroves that grew in abundance in this swampy wetland.

Gliding storks swooped down toward the water until their reflecting mirror images almost touched. Sometimes a wingtip would dip softly into the warm waters, causing ripples that persuaded the water lilies to move to a slow motion dance. The mangrove branches were the nesting homes for these storks as hundreds of these white giants could be seen perched and preening in the warmth and sunshine of the morning.

In various little coves, fishermen who worked the waters of the mangroves could be seen as they stood in their small carved-out boats, skillfully throwing nets and catching fish to support their livelihood. Often there were two fishermen in a boat. One man would guide the small launch by using a long pole in a similar fashion to the Venetian sailors who pilot the gondolas. The other fisherman would be balancing with one foot on the gunwale of the launch, while the other man was in the prow of the small craft. They made this tightrope walk look easy and performed it while pulling up the fishnet, then throwing it out into the water, over, and over, again.

As the replica of the African Queen docked, we gathered ourselves and climbed into the back of a pickup truck that doubled as an Island taxi. We then made our way through the semi-jungle landscape towards the ocean.

The children found the adventure invigorating. Their constant expressions of delight were clearly heard over the groans of the motor and squeaking of the suspension that complained after hitting every pothole on the four-wheel drive we moved along on.

Not ducking in time resulted in our faces being slapped as the low palm and banana tree leaves reached out to envelop whoever was not on guard. As the trees began to thin out, there was the scent of salted air and the delightful sound of breakers crashing a shore just over the next rise.

Finally arriving at the Pacific Ocean on Guatemala's coast, we found ourselves gawking in all directions at the sparkling black volcanic sand that formed the beach and stretched for miles to the north and south to unknown lands. Steam-like mist rose from the beach as the waves finished their trans-Pacific journey by celebrating their arrival with a mighty clap and foaming crash upon shore.

Hot and light wind gusts blew comfortable warmth all over us. A distance off the shoreline there were small thatched roofs, three and five-room cabanas with cooking facilities. The cabanas' courtyards supported shady spots with hammocks and a small swimming pool for freshwater lovers. This allowed us to settle in for the whole day and meet the needs that would arrive because we were nine adults, accompanied by six children.

Earlier that morning fifteen family members left Guatemala City in three vehicles, filling them to full occupancy. Every spare spot was filled with paraphernalia that would be needed that day. From food hampers to change of clothing, we loaded up everything that would make the day's adventure special to all. Body surfing, castle building, juice drinking, sun tanning, beach running, and family kibitzing were fully swinging.

Healthy appetites were being built as the fun continued into mid-afternoon. Las Senoras of our clan had been busily preparing a smorgasbord of culinary delight. Tamarindo, melon and mango juices with ice quenched everyone's big thirst. Plates and bowls of tasty tortillas, flavoured salads and black bean dip were generously spread across the large banqueting table situated under the shade of the palm trees. Choices of salsa, hot or mild, added spice to the noticeable three large platters of spaghetti that were evenly placed on the long table. My father-in-law's home blended Guatemalan coffee, adding a sense of family tradition and value to this tasty meal that had a covenantal mood to it.

Conversations were hardy and jovial. Life was being celebrated with compliments on the wonderful meal and pronouncements of congratulations to the cooks were expressed. In this ambience, as the end to the afternoon came upon us, the meal continued as we nibbled on fruit and sweets. Afterward, while walking a long distance along the beach, I entered into an enjoyable relaxation and a time to reflect on each member of this interesting family that God had allowed me entrance into through marriage.

By early evening it was time to pack up and pick up everything we brought and head back the way we came. The pickup truck let us off at the dock as the long flat bottom boat arrived. The way back through the waterways in the mangroves had brought about a great calm to everyone.

Celeste, my Latin beauty, was staring out to see the waves caused by the motored launch roll over the water lilies. She expressed wonder at the way the flower heads went under and then came back to float again. Her sister, Chata, asked the owner of the craft to stop in the middle of a cluster of lilies so she could take one home with her. As one was brought up, the tangled root system was intricately woven. She was able to secure three of them and carefully put them in a large plastic bag containing some water. I leaned on the very front of the boat as we proceeded onward and watched the sun hovering over the western sky.

Upon reflection of how the water lilies were connected in order to survive, I noticed this was not unlike the family structure we lived in. The reason the lilies did well was because the root system did well. Our family members do well for the same reason. Through our very large and extended family, my children have the privilege of original grandparents on both sides, cousins galore, and uncles and aunts aplenty. The fabrics of our lives are knitted together with the uniqueness of each other, and in order to bloom we need the healthy support of our family root systems.

As I mused on this proverb of life, I looked back and could see all of the relatives with golden sun rays coloring their faces as the setting sun was being admired. At that moment I saw them as gold and was happy to be established in my heart as a welcomed, viable member of their lives and them in mine.

The importance of kinsmen had come home to me and the homecoming was sweet.

I have since returned to Monterico and again was filled with an enjoyable time in paradise on earth with its black sand and hot winds. But as we floated by the water lilies, I was amused in that I was happy to see them. The word 'family' had kept coming up in my heart and mind. Were these floating floral arrangements teasing me? I'm not sure, but I supposed God was saying He had made water lilies to remind me of how rich I am in this life to be part of a large, loving family.

Thank you, Lord, for your personal human gifts that you gave me.

Norm

Butterflies In Bloom

But ask the animals, and they will teach you, or the birds in the sky, and they will tell you; or speak to the earth, and it will teach you, or let the fish in the sea inform you. Which of all these does not know that the hand of the Lord has done this? In his hand is the life of every creature and the breath of all mankind. Job 12:7-10

As spring finally makes its slow arrival here, I am eagerly awaiting the fluttering of butterflies on my lilac blooms. It always seems to take forever for spring to get here, and then another eternity for summer. It always seems like we just get our pool open and it's already time to close it down for fall. The seasons are feeling shorter and shorter, and I don't know why that is. When I was a child, summer felt like it went on endlessly, and so did a long, hot day at the beach. Now I'm watching the days fly by and my life go along with it, and trying to hold on to every moment like it's my last. When I finally start seeing butterflies on the lilacs, it feels like all is right with the world!

I remember a beautiful day at the beach in Petoskey when suddenly I found myself the target of an enamored butterfly. It was fluttering around me, so I put my hand out to it, and it landed on my finger and then began to flutter and whirl around me, delicately brushing its colorful wings against my face and shoulders. We all stood there in the warm sand,watching this playful butterfly dance around me, and then broke into laughter as it finally flittered away. This was one of those moments that I wanted time to stop, and every time I look at those pictures, I just sink into that feeling of joy. Butterflies make me instantly happy every time I see one.

People say butterflies are a sign that a loved one who passed is visiting. I'm not sure I believe that, but I would like to think God gives us nature to heal our souls, and if a visit from a butterfly is what brings us joy or healing, then He will use a butterfly.

I've been thinking about the life cycle of a butterfly and all the steps it must go through in order to become a beautiful winged creature. A butterfly lays its eggs on a leaf that must be undisturbed long enough to become a caterpillar, then the caterpillar needs to eat and then transform into a chrysalis. It must be completely still so predators will leave it alone, and then it will eventually emerge as a butterfly with beautiful wings. Even after this, the wings need to dry and harden to ready it for flight. This metamorphosis takes about three weeks, but so much can happen between each stage, it's amazing butterflies survive at all.

There is a metamorphosis of people that we don't see as well. If you were to read some of my earlier writings, you may have one impression of me. If you read something I wrote from two years ago, you may have another. But if you read something from last month, you may get yet another. This doesn't mean I'm wishy-washy in my convictions, but it does show I'm capable of growth and change. I may have strong feelings and opinions on a Monday, but have a conversation with a wise person on a Tuesday and have a change in my views. I want to be more open and more willing to search out what God wants me to say instead of what I want to say. I invite opportunities to grow my perspective and knowledge, and I don't want to be stuck in wrong thinking if that's the case. But if a person is stuck seeing my caterpillar stage, they will never get to know me as a butterfly.

But when completeness comes, what is in part disappears. When I was a child, I talked like a child, I thought like a child, I reasoned like a child. When I became a man, I put the ways of childhood behind me. For now we see only a reflection as in a mirror; then we shall see face to face. Now I know in part; then I shall know fully, even as I am fully known 1Corinthians 13:10-12

Butterflies really take a big risk, and so should we. There are times we may need to hang in a quiet chrysalis and think about what we've said or done, what we've gone through, or how we presented ourselves. We may need to make some adjustments while we're sitting still, and risk looking dull and lifeless until we've set ourselves straight. We could get knocked off our branches, chewed up by predators,or even written off as ugly. But maybe those who really know us will understand that what we're dealing with is a tough life cycle of change, and our breakthrough is coming soon.

Love prospers when a fault is forgiven, but dwelling on it separates close friends. Proverbs 17:9

It makes me wonder how many people we are still thinking of as caterpillars because of something that happened years ago, and we haven't even given a thought that maybe they think differently now, and they've long flown that image we had. How many friends or family have we lost because we heard something we didn't like and we didn't care enough to stick around and get the rest of the story? To see the rest of their cycle through? How many mistakes have we made that we've fixed, but no one has seen our changes? If we're willing to give someone too many chances, why is it we're not willing to give another even one?

I have yet to completely find, let alone spread my wings every day. I have caterpillar days, chrysalis days, and sometimes even egg days. What I hope to find are other wet-winged butterflies who understand that life is a cycle of growth, and we don't always present our best days. I won't always say or even do the right or best thing, but I'm always willing to communicate if someone cares enough to ask me to clarify. Grace is a two-way gift that helps us to realize that others need the same understanding that we do in order to keep growing strong. We can help each other through every tough stage of life and it can be beautiful in the end.

Above all, keep loving one another earnestly, since love covers a multitude of sins. 1Peter 4:8

Jami

Fireflies

Its brilliance can still be seen if you close your eyes and muse of a summer night in Las Arena. We, that is my wife, two sons and relatives of all sorts were lounging and resting in hammocks hung in various locations around the large veranda that surrounded the ranch house. We could see the mango and tamarind trees swaying to the sparse breeze that occasionally gave relief to the humid, glistening leaves.

Our hunger had been satisfied by indulging on a roasted lamb that had been cooked and sizzled on an open pit of amber hot coals, with the added delicacies of freshly made tortillas that the elderly Mayan woman had slapped from hand to hand.

Her own rhythm that came from years of being the ranch house cook had made this action look easy. Hot chirmol salsa tickled the tongue with bursts of hot and wonderful flavour. Fruit and vegetables were sauteed in secret recipes handed down from great-grandmothers who smiled as they heard our exclamations of mmm! Wow! Oh! and may I have more please? It was a feast that made the heart glad.

As evening began to reveal its display of stars and planets, the moon made her entrance, presenting her fullness as one who would rule the sky this night. Its brightness was calling everyone to the river that meandered its way by the ranch house. Its call went out to all. "Venga, venga vamos a el rio." We headed out on an evening adventure.

As we walked toward the river, the tall grass brushed across our legs giving goose bumps to the children because of a tickling sensation. It brought rushes to the older ones because of what they thought lingered in the tall grass. As we pressed on, we noticed fireflies offering themselves as beacons of light. The children squealed with delight and energy as they caught the mysterious bugs in their hands.

We waddled our way into the warm and slow-moving river. The span being about fifty feet and only waist high made this oasis a sense of welcome pleasure to enjoy in its fullest. The effect was spectacular as the moon moved behind the palm trees, causing silhouettes that gleamed and reflected the moon's shine. This reflection was also bouncing on the ripples caused by the water moving onward.

I moved toward my wife to steal a caress in this night of Latin moodiness. The water drops glistened on her caramel soft skin. The reflection of moonbeams moved from her eyes to mine, telling me I was hers. We frolicked and hugged each other, kissing eyelids and cheekbones with butterfly kisses.

In this moment of juvenile affection, we looked up the river to see the curvature of its banks overlaid with millions upon millions of fireflies. As far as the eye could see, whether up or down river, this panoramic view of nature was sparkling beyond belief. Creation was celebrating the love we had at that moment and gave approval of our union.

Silence overtook everyone as each person pondered their existence in this glorified moment. I am sure each person felt this vista had been manifested specifically for them as everyone drank in this feast for the eyes and soul.

Soon the children began to play and we

became human diving boards for them. Then we tossed them up river as far as we could, and then they would swim down towards us to do it again. I still remember this pure incantation. When I see water drops on my wife, I smile and think of the beauty of fireflies.

Norm

Take Me Where Your Heart Is

"Love seeks one thing only: the good of the one loved. It leaves all the other secondary effects to take care of themselves. Love, therefore, is its own reward." -Thomas Merton

Everything I've learned about love throughout my life has been through experience-trial, error, a little success, and lots of failure. Love is one of those things you can't learn or be by watching. It is an active, all hands-on, mind, soul, heart, and body invested, vulnerable immersion. Sometimes it feels like the biggest, warmest hug ever, and sometimes it leaves you completely shattered, tear-stained and broken, but the end result doesn't change. It's still love at the end, because love will always have its way. So was it really a failure? Maybe the desired outcome wasn't what I expected, but love did its job while it was there, and would I have changed anything if I could? That remains to be seen. Every experience in love has its meaning and regrets are a waste of time. **Love never fails.** 1Corinthians 13:8

As people, we can be fickle, narrow-minded, impatient, downright rude, and do I even need to say this-not always loving or even well-intentioned. Sometimes we rely selfishly on our opinions and our "feelings" instead of doing and saying what is right. We're not exactly reliable when it comes to following our hearts or even our brains! We've gotten ourselves lost so many times even the best GPS couldn't get us out! We make so many faux pas when it comes to relating with others. We can be sizzling hot messes at times. Prideful, angry, egotistical, right-fighting, unloving dolts.

But we were created by God because he wanted us-these completely imperfect beings. We were created by and for love, and Jesus died for us because He loved US. That is an amount of perfect love we cannot even grasp or measure. And even after all that, our imperfect love has a purpose too, and a great one at that. So even if we make mistakes in love, it can still turn out good because love has redemptive qualities, and we can show our vulnerability through those mistakes. When we let our guards down and put our hearts on the line, we can allow God's purpose to be seen through our messes. When we love like Jesus, it's a beautiful example of what God had in mind for us, because it reflects His love for us, and shows others how to love too. **Dear friends, let us love one another, for love comes from God. Everyone who loves has been born of God and knows God. Whoever does not love does not know God, because God is love. This is how God showed his love among us: He sent his one and only Son into the world that we might live through him.** 1John 4:7-9

Loving people can actually come fairly easy, but sometimes liking each other can be another story! I mean, just smile at me, and I will immediately like you. Make me laugh and it's instant love! Most of us are pretty easy to win over. It's the human part of us that looks to common interests and shared values to bond us together, and then we become friends. It's so easy to love our friends because they are like us, and it's not work to accept them. But we weren't asked to just love our friends. We were commanded to love people we don't like, and that includes enemies, and those horrible people "out there." **But I tell you, love your enemies and pray for those who persecute you, that you may be children of your Father in heaven. He causes his sun to rise on the evil and the good, and sends rain on the righteous and the unrighteous. If you love those who love you, what reward will you get?** Matthew 5:44-46

There are some things people do that are heinous and terrible, and we shrink at the thought of them, let alone loving people like that. But God loves us all, who can even fathom that kind of love? What does it look like to love each other when we are clearly living in a world full of evil? All I know is that the first One to put evil to rest was the love of God. If we are to love like Christ, then it makes sense to be compassionate when given the opportunity to love in those difficult situations. We have to remember that we are not alone in fighting the evil in the world. **Finally, be strong in the Lord and in his mighty power. Put on the full armor of God so that you can take your stand against the devil's schemes.** Ephesians 6:10-11 I probably say this too much, but our job is not to judge and prosecute other people. It is to love people, and when we do that, we are in a better position to change situations and help what is going on around us. Judgement only creates rigidness, where love creates flexibility, opportunity, and action. I despise evil and wrongdoing just as much as anyone does, but the source of evil should be our main target. **For our struggle is not against flesh and blood, but against the rulers, against the authorities, against the powers of this dark world and against the spiritual forces of evil in the heavenly realms.** Ephesians 6:12

Do you love people who don't love you back? I think most people can think of someone, whether family or friend, who we continue to reach for, and they prickle at our attempts. We can still love someone, even if it's not returned, because we were created to love, and love is at its heart, goodness and kindness. It doesn't matter if it is unwanted or unreturned, because the act of loving is something we are and not something we do. Just try to stop loving someone you love. It doesn't work that way, does it? We don't give love to someone to get something back, and if we are, then we need to reevaluate. If we're wanting returns on all our love investments, it has become conditional at some level. If pure love is always in our heart, we will always walk away having been what we set out to be, even if we walk away empty-handed or alone. We can still "seek the good of the one loved" and keep them in our prayers, even if they aren't in our physical lives.

Love is calm, deep, and soft-hearted, so that we can have the ability to forgive when it is hard. Love transforms us into gentler, more humble people, and gives us the confidence to be good to those who aren't good to us. Forgiveness allows us to move on and love again too, in due time. That's how powerful love can be, if we allow love and God to live fully in our hearts. **He answered, " 'Love the Lord your God with all your heart and with all your soul and with all your strength and with all your mind' and, 'Love your neighbor as yourself."** Luke 10:27

And I pray that you, being rooted and established in love, may have power, together with all the Lord's holy people, to grasp how wide and long and high and

deep is the love of Christ, and to know this love that surpasses knowledge-that you may be filled to the measure of all the fullness of God. Ephesians 3:17-19

Love should always make you better. It should always bring out the best version of you. It is self-disciplined, doing the right thing even when it's hard, and is honest and kind. It is compassionate, thoughtful, considerate, willing to listen and willing to communicate and comprehend, and determined to seek peace in all situations. Love is patient and it is persistent. While it may retreat, it never gives up, because love is strong on its own even when it isn't loved in return. It is trusting and protective of itself and its own, and protects others. Love admits mistakes, corrects them, and seeks forgiveness as well as forgives. Love will sacrifice without a second thought. Love wants you to be closer to God, and will pull you closer to Him. Love is patient and love never fails. The love of people may fail us, but God's love never will. God IS love.

Jami

----- *The Line of Colour*-----

I thought of colouring books and western scenes, there in a flash a long past dream. A memory alive I remember the smell of crayon upon pictures coloured pastel. Fast running horses and Indians aflight, with purple and orange feathers and rust coloured guns. Colouring my best to stay within the lines till finally with heart the drawing was done. Now I colour life with payments on house, tulip garden and loving spouse, bringing up babies to stand as men to choose colours that make mankind friends. It hasn't changed much - life and time. We still try to colour within the lines.

Norm

More Than A Love Song

"Music is the language of the spirit. It opens the secret of life bringing peace, abolishing strife." -Kahlil Gibran

It's almost Valentine's Day, and whether or not you believe in or even care about celebrating the so-called "Hallmark holiday", I believe in celebrating love every day, and if I could, I would eat chocolate every day too! I'm a real sucker for all things love! I want it all-real life love stories about people finding each other after years of separation, sappy movies about love, poetry, and my personal favorite, songs about love! Lest we all forget my penchant for finding heart shapes in ordinary objects- it's still happening! At the center of all things love is the One who made love possible in us at all, because He IS love-God. **We love because He first loved us.** 1John 4:19

As the title of one of Leo Buscaglia's books in my collection reads, Love-What Life is All About. A sign in my home says, "*Love makes everything better.*" That's my theory too- it makes everything better, but does anything else really matter without it? Can we have peace without it? Hope? Forgiveness? It all begins with and is fueled by love. A love for someone or a love for something. And yet there are so many deterrents to love. So many enemies of love. So many obstacles between people, between us and God, us and the ones close to us. Love isn't just a sweet song, sappy movie, or fuzzy feeling on Valentine's Day. It requires action above any words, any grand gesture, candy or roses. It sometimes requires pain and selflessness, and doing things we don't want to do or think we can do. **For God so loved the world that he gave his one and only Son, that whoever believes in him shall not perish but have eternal life.** John 3:16 Jesus is the ultimate example of sacrifice,suffering, selflessness, and giving beyond limits for the love of us all. Simple love is an action, sometimes with no words necessary at all. Consistent, persistent, evident love. I think of parental love when I think of this type of love. Many times we think our kids aren't hearing us, and maybe they aren't, but they can see us, and they can certainly know our love by our consistent actions.

"Just because the message may never be received does not mean it is not worth sending." Segaki

If we've decided to be one of those risk-takers who love people, because if we're honest, that's what love is- taking a risk. We risk losing a part of ourselves every time we love. So if we decide to love, we also decide to take whatever comes with it, even if that means a potential loss, an unheard message, or a heartache. We hand over our hearts and trust someone or something else with it, knowing the benefits of love are so amazing, but the chance of pain-is it worth it? You can't really have one without the other, can you? You can't really love someone without trusting them with your heart. If you're not willing to take that risk, you're really risking so much more than a heartbreak. You're risking never knowing what it's like to be loved or to love with a person like that. You have to go all in, because if you're going to be mediocre about love, then you may also get a mediocre result.

"Love is always open arms. If you close your arms about love you will find that

you are left holding only yourself." Leo Buscaglia, LOVE, What Life is All About....

The beauty of love is that even when there is heartache or rejection, we find that if we allow ourselves to be tenderized by that pain, we will grow into a more deeply loving person. If we allow ourselves to become embittered by heartache, we will be less tolerant of the pain of others, and less compassionate to the needs around us. We will grow complacent, and hardened to the love others may try to give us. So is love worth it even if it hurts in the end? Yes. That will always be the answer. Because the love we give is always worth it. The message is always worth sending! Loving is rarely going to be about what we receive back, but about our impact on someone else. If we think about love in this way, we can take heartache and let it heal us instead of tearing us down. **Love one another. As I have loved you.** John 13:34

"**Where words fail, music speaks**."- Hans Christian Andersen

Thank God for songs to express the things some of us can't say to each other or to Him! **"Music is a gift and grace of God, not an**

invention of men."-Martin Luther. When I heard Andrea Bocelli sing "Con Te Partiro" for the first time, it reminded me of how I felt when I heard "Ave Maria" in a beautiful old church. It was a heart-touching song in a different language than my native English, and moved me to unexpected tears. When I listen to praise and worship music, it draws me closer to God. **So what shall I do? I will pray with my spirit, but I will also pray with my mind; I will sing with my spirit, but I will also sing with my mind.** 1Corinthians 14:15 Sometimes we can let a song speak to someone for us, or let the melody draw out our words, as I do when I am writing. Music is used for celebrating, worshipping, healing and for connecting. If music is a gift and grace of God, then let it be used abundantly and well.

Let's look around and pay attention to the people God has given us to love! We all should know that tomorrow isn't promised. Apologize when necessary, forgive often, and do the hard things, because when we act out of true, selfless love, we become the most powerful force in anyone's life, especially our own.

"Love recognizes no barriers. It jumps hurdles, leaps fences, penetrates walls to arrive at its destination full of hope."- Maya Angelou

Jami

Part two:

Peace

Peace: It's All About Us

Let your gentleness be evident to all. The Lord is near. Philippians 4:5

In a world where war, civil disputes, serious crime, and conflicts are constant and inevitable, we are surrounded by viciousness, violence, and hate. Because of instant technology, we have access to violence and anger updates 24/7 on our phones, in our homes, and at our jobs. If someone famous, or anyone really, makes a terrible gaffe at 9am, the entire world will know about it by noon the same day. We are inundated with bad news and gossip if we allow ourselves to engage. And even if we try not to, someone will most likely inform us of something we don't even care to know. We don't have to engage in every discussion we are invited to, remembering some people just want to vent their frustrations, and few want to hear solutions.

This is what the Lord Almighty said: 'Administer true justice; show mercy and compassion to one another. Do not oppress

the widow or the fatherless, the foreigner or the poor. Do not plot evil against each other.' Zechariah 7:9-10

Jesus was the example of true justice, mercy, and compassion. He put us above His own interests, and we weren't exactly the examples of great friends and family when He did that for us. He gave all of his life so that we could have any life of our own at all, let alone any of those rights, privileges, and ambitions we are always squawking on about. We complain about all the negativity in the world, but don't even realize that we are becoming the bullhorn and billboard for it as we repeat it over and over. We sometimes get so stuck on ourselves and our own selfish ways that we forget the state of others altogether. We forget to ask someone how they are doing before we dump a load of garbage on them. We forget to consider that not everyone sees something the same way we do, and therefore may not respond in the same way, and get annoyed at them. We get tunnel vision easily when we are all about ourselves and our own interests. Not only do we forget others, but we forget God too.

Once we take our eyes away from ourselves, from

our interests, from our own rights, privileges, ambitions-then they will become clear to see Jesus around us. Mother Teresa

2020 was a time when mob mentality became stronger for some than family and friendship ties. When people began to bond over hating the same things, instead of loving the same thing. It's never a true connection to just jump into a group of strangers and hate on something together, though people who don't have something more solid to hold onto may find it's the best connection they've ever had. If we are in Christ together and being who He says we are, then we would not be hating at all, but finding our way back to each other in a way that glorifies Him. If we love Him and if we love each other-that's the key, or at least the beginning. When you begin to put your own interests above the people you say you love, you no longer consider that person. They become collateral damage in your quest to prove something that is clearly more important to you than them.

Love the Lord your God with all your heart and with all your soul and with all your strength and with all your mind and

love your neighbor as yourself. Luke 10:27

That is not just a command, but also an individual decision that we each need to make in order to have true and meaningful relationships with others, and common respect among strangers. (Yes, I just referred to love as a decision, because it is) Anything else we may forge will eventually break and be floating on the surface. If we are not rooted in Christ, we will be uprooted at the first signs of a storm. This is how my friendships were tested in 2020. One would survive, and one would not. God was in one, but not the other. **Do nothing out of selfish ambition or vain conceit. Rather in humility value others above yourselves, not looking to your own interests but each of you to the interests of others.** Philippians 2:3-4

My decades-long friendship went off the rails after a few exchanges that finally resulted in a complete derailment and fire. Looking back, I would have engaged much differently, however, at the time I allowed my emotions, ego, and pride to do as they pleased. All of those things, when combined with those of another, will never result in a positive conversation or resolution of any kind. God was not invited to the conversation. Big mistake. At that point, it was two people speaking into the wind, going in opposite tornadic directions. I couldn't blame the other person for choosing not to respond to me ever again. What I was hoping to accomplish was one thing, but my wounded self said another. My wounded self always says things she shouldn't say! Wounds are not reliable representatives for words, or for anything, for that matter.

I've done similar things with friends in the past. I haven't always had the best relationship skills. I didn't always know the Lord and even when I did, I didn't always ask for His help. I was defensive, insecure, wore my heart on my sleeve, and was very prideful. My wounded ego caused me to be hurt easily, so even if told the truth, I wouldn't take it well. How can I fault someone for reacting the exact same way I have done in the past? I used to be like hugging a porcupine, quills at the ready. I found comfort hiding behind the huge brick wall that I had fearfully built around myself. I was the one smiling with my arms folded to keep everyone out and then crying because they left.

I understand being protective of yourself and fighting hard for the things you believe. Until I met God and let Him guide and love that wild, untamed part of me. So,with grace and love, I should have been the one to know better how to speak, respond, and let things go, but I let my reactive wounds talk instead because I was speaking out of sheer hurt and rejection and a mixture of shock and disappointment. I also know that when God allows someone to walk out the door without looking back, and without even a question after so much history, maybe God was holding the door.

For our struggle is not against flesh and blood, but against the rulers, against the authorities, against the powers of this dark world and against the spiritual forces of evil in the heavenly realms. Ephesians 6:12

We weren't actually fighting about political sides, masks, the government, or any other hot-button pandemic issue. I care about my friends regardless of their positions on any of those things. We were fighting against the very things that were put there in order to cause division among us all. They were angry and fearful and so was I, but about completely opposite things, and I no longer recognized my friend as someone I even knew, and that was the element I was fighting. I was fighting someone I could no longer find a common ground with, and it scared me. They no longer saw my decades of trust, my acceptance, my respect, or any of the good they once believed in. Where they had once referred to me as an "angel" and a "saint" of a friend, I was now being seen as an adversary, and there was nothing I could say or do to change that. That was so confusing to me. I could no longer find that comfortable place of peace with this person and it was unsettling to me. Rather than continue to subject myself to this fearful position, I found that it was time to exit in order to remain peaceful. It broke my heart, but that describes the whole of 2020 for me and a lot of people, I think.

If it is possible, as far as it depends on you, live at peace with everyone. Romans 12:18

One thing we can't control is others' perception of how they receive what we've said, especially if we aren't given a chance to discuss it at all. So much can be cleared up and put to rest in a simple conversation. Something that has been fiercely difficult for me to learn through this experience is that no matter how much we want explanations or closure in a situation, we are not always owed that, and even if we think we are, we may not always have the benefit of that. What I may believe could heal the situation or help me understand may not even matter to the other person, and so we have to just pick up and move on. This is one of those situations where grace steps in and allows me to put the band-aid on the blister and wait for it to heal, understanding that others will not always be involved in helping us heal the wounds they may have salted. We may not be 100% responsible for the rub, but we are responsible for our own healing. Part of that healing is being willing to be apologetic, take accountability for my part, forgive the other person for theirs, and ask God to work out the rest. We should always desire to be at peace with everyone with whom we interact. This is how we show the light of Christ.

The soothing tongue is a tree of life, but a perverse tongue crushes the spirit.

Proverbs 15:4

We can trust God for healthy relationships and for positive interactions. We can ask Him to guide our conversations with outsiders. It has been a difficult season of engaging with others. This experience served me well only in that it shed light on the fact that gentleness is not only a better way to approach others, but it is necessary. In a time when people aren't agreeing about some very hot topic items, we need to be aware that our words can not only offend, but they can also heal. Even though I am sad about the broken friendship, I realize that in trusting God for my relationships, there is a purpose for every bad experience we go through with people too. We may have been the ones hurt or the ones doing the hurting, but what is done with that pain going forward is what will show up in our character going forward.

It is imperative to have a friend you can trust, and someone that can not only speak truth into your life, but someone who also allows you to speak truth into theirs. My dear friend Norm became my dear friend because he cut through my garbage and told me the truth.

He told me the truth because he cared about me and the state of my life and trusted that I would receive it. In accepting that wisdom and accountability, the friendship grew, and so did my knowledge of myself and my faith. It can be intimidating if you allow your pride to intercept that wisdom speaking into your life and you're still wanting to white-knuckle your way through it on your own. But it can be very freeing to listen and put new action into place when someone who is succeeding in life wants to see you succeed too. It is a rare find to have a friend who tells you the truth these days, or to be allowed to speak truth to someone. We have to humble ourselves if we ever want to grow and become better, and honestly, to have real and meaningful relationships with others. I thank God that Norm listens to the Lord and relays His word to me. That is how I can trust Norm's wise and humble guidance. As Norm puts it, our friendship holds up to God's scrutiny because God is also in the friendship. My advice to any who may be going through a friendship trial is to do as I've been doing, just pray for that person. It's really a very loving thing to do for anyone. We may be in a period of silence right now, but I do want to see this person happy and blessed in every area of life.

One who has unreliable friends soon comes to ruin, but there is a friend who sticks closer than a brother. Proverbs 18:24

It won't be our viciousness in how we fight for things, our hills we die on, our stubbornness and firmly planted feet, that will show how much we believe in a thing or love a person. It will be our gentleness, our tenderness, and our willingness to be humble and soft at a time when it would be easier to be ferocious and self-righteous. We need to understand that "keeping the peace" doesn't mean being quiet. It means knowing when to speak and with the wisdom you've attained from God, how to speak it with love. To allow a person to be who they are, while still loving them enough to confront a negative behavior because you actually care about their peace and well-being too. And if you get pushback, to be able to leave your pride at the door and let the results rest with God. That's the peace we can all have when we let God be the light in us.

You are the light of the world. A town built on a hill cannot be hidden. Neither

do people light a lamp and put it under a bowl. Instead they put it on its stand, and it gives light to everyone in the house. In the same way, let your light shine before others, that they may see your good deeds and glorify your Father in heaven. Matthew 5:14-16

Jami

Six Pieces of The Puzzle

Proverbs 25:2 It is God's privilege to conceal things and the king's privilege to discover them.

When I stop at the library to drop off or pick up the items I have ordered, I sometimes head over to the puzzle tables to see what progress has been made. There are four tables next to huge windows filtering ambient light upon the puzzles at different stages of completion. People who drop in at the library often sit at these tables finding pieces to the puzzles and after they have found and placed a few pieces they move on. Then other library visitors sit down to do the same. This morning while I was at the library, I sat alone at a puzzle and found six pieces that fit. I then moved on to other things I had to do. I had done my part to expose the picture coming to completion on that table. My six pieces opened up an area of discovery that others could build upon.

Isn't that what we do as we live our lives?

We are born into the citizenry of this earth by God's will for a certain dispensation of time to fit our pieces of the puzzle into the lifelong picture and story of life. We were created on purpose, with a purpose, and for a purpose that the Lord ordained, and we each have a piece of the puzzle that others need so that we can all finish the plan God has for us. It is our human right as created beings to find the mysteries of life and rejoice with God when we find them. With His wisdom, our Heavenly Father gives us the sagacity to track down, discover, and search them out. Proverbs 25:2 **It is God's privilege to conceal things and the king's privilege to discover them.**

We all have a part to play in the big picture of eternity because God has placed eternity in our hearts. Ecclesiastes 3:11a **He has made everything beautiful in its time. He has also set eternity in the human heart**. The Lord has been putting together a life plan for us and we need to discover where and how to be part of it. At the same time, we must understand that we are replaceable. If we do not step up to the responsibility of our calling in life, then someone else will. God pointed out to Elijah that there were seven thousand others who had not bowed their knee to Baal, even though Elijah thought he was the only faithful servant God had. 1Kings 19:18 **Nevertheless, I have reserved seven thousand in Israel—all whose knees have not bowed to Baal and whose mouths have not kissed him**. Other people in Elijah's time were also putting God's plan to work for the sake of mankind.

Since we are soldiers in the Lord's army, as the scriptures reason, then we are part of a much bigger picture and we are a piece of the strategy needed to bring the kingdom of God's reign on this earth. We would be wise to focus on what the Master of our soul is doing within us and pay attention to His directions so that we do not get caught up in the trivia of the world. 2Timothy 2:4 **No soldier gets entangled in civilian pursuits, since his aim is to please the one who enlisted him**. In like manner, as stated in the second Corinthians chapter five verses 18 and 19, we are ministers of reconciliation, therefore, we have a piece of the healing puzzle that people need to be reconciled to God, themselves, and one another. We have Jesus in our hearts, the healer of nations.

We are described as God's hand extended in this world. That description brings eternal responsibility to our lives. We are to wield the weapons of righteousness that God has given us to accomplish the Lord's will in His Kingdom. This is why we yield to the Holy Spirit, to accomplish what God has instructed us to do. Therefore, obeying God and finding the pieces of the puzzle needed to bring the blessings of God to a lost world is a privilege we walk in. We are kings and priests who serve the Lord and have the blessed opportunity to seek out the mysteries God has appointed us to solve. Revelation 1:6 **And hath made us kings and priests unto God and his Father; to Him be glory and dominion for ever and ever. Amen.**

As we continue going forward in life and keep placing the pieces of the puzzle we have figured out, let us help those who are stuck with difficult pieces to assemble. Some people are very good at solving the most laborious puzzles and can move along quickly in snapping the pieces into place. Others are not sure and take meticulous time to place each piece forward, backward, sideways, and at every angle imaginable. They seem to take forever to place one piece, but then, there it is, in place. It may have been the most important piece of the puzzle. The key is to keep looking at where we fit and where we belong in the grand picture of the Lord's invention. Let us be the piece that fits the situation bringing peace to us all. In Jesus name!

Norm

Conquering Denise

One Sunday evening, I was making everyone a fun dessert of chocolate cake waffle sundaes. I can never remember how much batter to pour onto the waffle iron, but of course, I followed the "instructions" and confidently poured 2 cups of chocolate cake batter onto the hot iron and closed the lid. Not even two seconds later, the goopy chocolate batter began to ooze out of three sides of the maker and down onto the controls and the countertops. Alarmed, I began commanding it to "Stop it! No! Don't do that! Whoa! No No No!!!" in my most authoritative voice, while also scooping up the oozing batter with a paper towel and a paper plate, and my hands.

Apparently, my mom thought it was pretty funny, as she "helped" by putting her hysterical face in her hands and her head down onto the countertop, but my sidekick Serena jumped in to rescue me as the chocolate river continued to flow. She became my waffle sous chef and advisor, who just kept helping direct the impressive lava and the removal of the cooked waffles. The addition of Steve's "Lucyyyy.. you've got some 'splainin' to doooo" just added to my mom's inability to get ahold of herself. The antics continued, as I momentarily lost my spatula and tongs and could not remove the waffles from the iron when the beeper went off. This created a near collision, as I turned to Steve, reaching into the sink where he had just put them. I guess my yelling, "Where? Where? Why?" and "What the heck?" did little for others to realize I needed assistance with my untensil location. Flailing and spinning about helplessly while spewing nonsense was more entertaining, I suppose. Not one to disappoint with my improv routines, I added a little extra fun to the scene with my natural dance moves.

You would think a little thing like making dessert for my family would be simple. I have actually made this before! But one little slip up caused a chain of ridiculousness that actually ended up being the most fun we had all day. In case you're wondering, you place those wonderful chocolate waffles on a plate, put a scoop of vanilla ice cream on top. Drizzle (more like dump) on some hot fudge sauce, add some whipped cream and some sprinkles. It's so good! Side note, two cups of batter is about one cup too many, but don't take my word for it. Clearly, I don't know what I'm doing.

As I reflected on this moment later, I thought about how often I do these kinds of silly things and have to humor and finagle my way through them. I wonder if God looks at me like the chocolate ooze and says, "No No NO, Don't do that! Stop it! Whoa!" even as He fixes my problem mercifully. Much like my servant-hearted daughter, Serena, who jumped in without judgment to help save the day, or should I say, the countertop, and maybe my pride? She does have restaurant management experience, and boy, did she show her skills. Me as a chef? Not so much that day. More like the Swedish chef from the Muppets!

I make a lot of mistakes. But I try a lot of things that are probably out of my wheelhouse and sometimes even my energy to do. Before I had restrictions to lift and move furniture, I used to move all kinds of heavy, bulky furniture with no help. When Steve would get home, he would look around and say suspiciously, "Where did the…what did you DO… and how...?" Well, I figured out how to improvise, that's what I did, and I still do! If I want something done, and there's no one around to help me, I figure it out. God must have a good laugh at me now and then, when He sees me cooking up yet another idea or figuring out how to do what seems difficult or impossible at first. I am very determined when I get something in my mind to do.

I don't like relying on other people. I want to fix everything myself! It also annoys me that I have irrational fears that stop me from doing things, like raking unknown piles of leaves, because I just "know" there are snakes in them. I just know it! Ironically, snakes show up right in the middle of a mowed lawn where everyone is parked in lawn chairs visiting too, so some situations just can't be eliminated. I also want to conquer my fear of the chainsaw, but that could be trouble too. I do enjoy (and generally need) all of my attached limbs very much.

Some mishaps can't be avoided either, and to avoid things like messy waffle explosions would have meant missing out on a kitchen full of laughter. I haven't laughed about that snake yet, and I probably never will, but life is about turning mishaps and mistakes into memories sometimes. In fact, getting back to that furniture moving reference, I have trapped myself in stairways a few times trying to move large objects that became wedged somehow, and I just had to resolve that I was going to have to live in the basement forever, trapped by an ugly old bookcase. I named her Denise. She isn't the first to trap me and she won't be the last. When I finally wedged her loose and slid her where I wanted her to go, it was cause for celebration. (Cue the Rocky Balboa music) Every moment we persevere, we prove to ourselves that we can keep going even through all the "Denises" in our way.

Life just isn't that funny on its own. It can be pretty messy and pretty hard and sad sometimes. We all know this feeling. We have to look for our own joy and create our own entertainment, because the world isn't going to give it to us for free. The people who love and support us are going to laugh us through the waffle messes, help us clean them up, or just tease us mercilessly. Hopefully they'll rid us of the snakes, help us move the heavy stuff, and move us out of the way of things that threaten to crush our spirits.

Our family has had its share of hardships and illness, but one thing we all know how to do well is find the humor in most situations, and that has been the secret to our success and our survival. Make the best of it, remember the good times, and laugh when you can. Life isn't funny, but we can always find a reason to smile.

Jami

Little Foxes

Proverbs 4:6 Forsake her not, and she shall preserve thee: love her, and she shall keep thee.

Song of Songs 2:15 **Catch for us the foxes—the little foxes that ruin the vineyards—for our vineyards are in bloom.**

Although the little foxes in the case of the above scripture verse is referring to the little things that can destroy a loving relationship or a marriage - we can also see this analogy as ruining our love relationship with God who loves us fully. Romans 5:8 **But God proves his own love for us in that while we were still sinners, Christ died for us.** If we do not stay close to God, the little things that distract us and leave us vulnerable to sin can take the bloom off of our love for God. Self-condemnation and guilt can cause us to step back from crying out to God for His forgiving love.

It is the little things that bring tension into a marriage as in intimacy issues, debt, illness, broken promises, careless statements or taking one another for granted. These things are not evil in themselves, but these little foxes can get in the way of married life when our attention is drawn away from our lovers because of all these looming issues. Love is gentle and delicate; therefore, must be nurtured by being aware of the little foxes that can cause problems within an honest and heartfelt union of love.

The separation of loved ones is the enemy's tactic, and it is not always a full blown frontal assault that he uses to undermine and destroy relationships. Most of the time it is the small things that are piled one on top of another that start to wear out the heart's capacity to go forward in love - causing a stale and loveless existence. Revelation 2:4 **Nevertheless I have somewhat against thee, because thou hast left thy first love.**

When the little foxes are caught and dealt with before trouble starts, then love is vibrant and full of God's power, giving us the supernatural ability to be the first to apologize, forgive, and extend love because the love is nurtured and genuine. Someone once said, "The first to apologize is the bravest. The first to forgive is the strongest. The first to forget is the happiest." No wonder the enemy of our soul tries to break up lovers' closeness and intimacy.

The reason for the attack on Christian couples is simple. A husband and wife, who together love and serve the Lord by faith, are a force to be reckoned with. Satan knows it to be true and this is why he spends so much time being a home wrecker. Ecclesiastes 4:12 **A person standing alone can be attacked and defeated, but two can stand back-to-back and conquer. Three are even better, for a triple-braided cord is not easily broken.**

When a husband and wife are covenanted with God and are in union, the triple-braided cord will strangle the works of the enemy. Matthew 18:18 **Truly I tell you, whatever you bind on earth will have been bound in heaven, and whatever you loose on earth will have been loosed in heaven.** 19 **Again, truly I tell you, if two of you on earth agree about any matter that you pray for, it will be done for you by my Father in heaven.**

Yes, the little foxes ruin the vineyards, and the little things we ignore when God's voice is talking to us can affect the strength of our faith because we start taking God for granted. Remember, the lover of our soul is God Himself, and not some philanderer who uses and throws us aside when He is bored with us. No, Saints. He is the one who gave His son, Jesus, as a living sacrifice because His love was and is absolutely real toward us. We can count on the love of God for now and evermore. Jeremiah 31:3 **The LORD has appeared of old to me, saying: "Yes, I have loved you with an everlasting love; Therefore with lovingkindness I have drawn you."** Time to chase the little foxes away for good. Amen!

Norm

I Wonder Why

I wonder why pain must be the darkness
that leads us to the light,
Why heartbreak lends to healing,
and love can make us fight.
How do we hold on to someone tightly
Never dreaming we'll let go,
But let them slip right through our grasp
Hiding feelings they'll never know.
I wonder why we learn from ashes,
but not the fire as it burns,
We don't speak the word or take the time,
It's so hard for us to learn.
Why do we close our eyes so tight
to remember,
but can't see with open eyes
I wonder why.

Jami

Wow, What A Ride!

We had risen early one December holiday morning and ventured on the idea of some tobogganing, in order to burn up some energy that had been consumed during the time off from school and the sugar season that comes every year near the end of December. We dressed in the appropriate bulkiness of winter garb and headed out in pursuit of our favourite Chrysler of hills. On the way the boys talked and voiced with great enthusiasm the maneuvers and techniques they would use to conquer the perceived challenge set before them. We had gathered the usual toboggans, slippery mats, and the king of all sliding transport, a big inner-tube. As we pulled up and parked the car, we could see the hill, bright, white, and huge, with no one on it. How delightful the fresh smell of pine forest and the sound of light gusts of winter wind that sporadically loosened clusters of collected snow on the high green boughs, causing a spray of snow to float downward, giving life to the forest that flanked the toboggan runs. The clear visibility was to be enjoyed and viewed through the eyes of children. We all made our way to the top and with different modes of snow gear we hurled down the hill as fast as we could go. Faster and faster we went, in order to get as close as we could to the frozen pond.

The morning activities had begun to wear out the boys as they had gone downhill many times using different degrees of skill, from standing on the toboggan to laying stomach first, conquering everything as they tried to balance. "Well this is the last run boys, what do we do?" "Lets all get in the tube together!" said the boys in harmony. I placed myself in the middle and one son on each side of me and we hugged close and tight. With a small push, we started to move slowly, but not for long, because within seconds we were moving down and started to spin around at the same time. The sound of the tube on the snow was that of a rocket picking up speed, the wind in our faces was frosty, the slightest bump caused immediate lift and our grips on each other were fast loosening. We were headed for the pond and that is when we hit the edge of it, which caused us all to fly off the tube in different directions. Thump, wham, puff. We landed in a large cluster of frozen reeds. After a quick inventory to see if all personal parts were in place, we noticed that we were covered in a cloud of what seemed to be goose down but ended up being bullrush heads that had exploded when we crashed into them. We were covered in feather-like seeds floating all about us . As we tried to spit them out of our mouths we broke into a crescendo of laughter at each other because we looked like we had been tarred and feathered. Head to foot, all you could see were soft seeds pasted to everything we were wearing. "Wow what a ride ah! dad" said Troy with sparkles in his eyes as Adam just continued to laugh and laugh. We made our way to the car and tried to clean up, but found it impossible, so we put our coats in the trunk with the winter sliding gear and drove homeward smiling broadly as I listened to the boys give an account of what had happened to us over and over and over again with joyful laughter accompanying the story.

This is one of the boys favourite memories and once in a while one of them will say, "Do you remember the time we all landed in the bullrushes, what a ride ah!?"

Norm

The Battle

Darkness, my enemy, the hours long,
When hands are heavy and peace is gone.
The moonlit sky is not for sleeping,
Thoughts become memories, none worth keeping.
My heart keeps uneven time in my chest,
My mind is torn from east to west.
Blackness heaves walls where light can shatter,
The enemy creeps, his lies shred and tatter.
The battle rages, heart and mind,
"you're no good- a mess- far from kind..."
Over and over, mistakes I've made
the words cutting and tearing with
his evil blade.
Then I remember who I was made to be,
The person God remade into me.
"Our Father..." it is done,
and the darkness recedes.
He hears my worship and His presence bleeds.
I return to peace and slumber is mine,
I settle in Truth and rest in the Divine.

Jami

Balanced

But the fruit of the Spirit is love, joy, peace, forbearance, kindness, goodness, faithfulness, gentleness, and self-control. Against such things there is no law. Galatians 5:22-23

In my quest to find out the secret of what makes people "happy", I noticed that happy people know how to keep their lives in a healthy state of proportion. Have you ever heard the phrase, "everything in moderation?" It's kind of the same thing. It means there is an intentional effort to maintain a healthy amount of each of the elements of our lives. Work, home, family, relationships, rest, community, etc... We all have responsibilities and interests of all different kinds and trying to keep up with them all at the same time can be exhausting and challenging. I call it "juggling and trying to keep all the balls up in the air." Drop one ball and all of them come tumbling down. There is a sense of anxiety and stress about juggling, though, and life doesn't have to be that way if we insert a sense of intention into every area of what we commit ourselves to. It's easy to get overwhelmed if we don't know how to prioritize or eliminate the things that don't need our commitment or attention. If we are working too much, our families may begin to suffer from our absence. If we spend too much time shopping, our bank accounts as well as our time may get out of balance. If we are worrying, fretting, complaining, and venting, we are going to find ourselves out of balance emotionally and probably affect the balance in our relationships. If we begin to isolate ourselves socially, we will soon find ourselves out of balance where any relationships are concerned. A lack of balance can create havoc anywhere-our physical health from a lack of exercise or medical attention, our marriages from a lack of time or from too much arguing, our bodies from too much stress, too much eating, not enough water, and sometimes not enough rest and quiet time. And certainly, not enough time with God and hearing what He has to say to us. God will always want us to put Him first, and when we do that, all other things will fall into place. **But seek first His**

kingdom and his righteousness, and all these things will be given to you as well. Matthew 6:33 I don't know how many times I have caught myself flustered and sputtering about something, and didn't stop to pray about it first. God will bring balance to a life that nothing and no one else can. He says, **"Be still, and know that I am God; I will be exalted among the nations, I will be exalted in the earth."** Psalm 46:10

I believe a happy person is one who knows their own limitations, respects their own time and that of others, and knows how to form the word, "NO." Spreading ourselves out too thin in order to please everyone else is a great way to get out of balance, and also a way to build up resentment when you're not really doing things out of the spirit in your own heart.

It is a balanced person (not a perfect one) who will strive to prioritize their spiritual life, family life, work duties, home care, personal desires, community life, and still manage to find time for others when the need arises, because it allows for hiccups and emergencies to occur. A person in balance generally uses their time well, so they have a better sense of what they can give to others.

Balance allows for wiggle room, because we won't try to cram too many things into our lives that we don't really have time for. A person who is balanced also values and uses time wisely. Remember that teacher back in grade school who used to write that on the report card-"uses time wisely"? Well, I was a daydreamer in some of my classes, so there was that. I didn't do well in the classes where I couldn't balance my daydreaming time with my listening time!

A balanced person takes time for self-care as well as time for hobbies. I don't believe this comes naturally to most people. Some of us can't tell ourselves "no" when it comes to working, and some of us just can't relax. There are a lot of guilt-ridden people who believe they aren't allowed to enjoy themselves! The Lord has given us talents and gifts that we are to share with others and yes, for our personal enjoyment too. Some of us need to be disciplined to work more, and some of us need to learn to play more! There are many areas of our lives that could use some equilibrium, and it's for our own benefit that we should keep striving for that. We are a very unbalanced group of humans sometimes, but with God's help, we can overcome ourselves. **No discipline seems pleasant at the time, but painful. Later on, however, it produces a harvest of righteousness and peace for those who have been trained by it.** Hebrews 12:11

Jami

A Constitution With A Constellation

Tonight offered a welcome breeze to think in shades and smells of melancholy. Gazing up I saw an old friend hadn't seen half a cycle.

Norm: Orion you look astronomically brilliant. Where have you been?

Orion: I've been rolling over the Northern sphere. The Aurora Borealis was so nice this year. My feet have been moving below the equator to continue my existence as the great crusader. I've come to impress the Southern Cross, That in all my travels I never get lost. And now my friend I'll talk to you,

Sincerely Norm, how do you do?

Norm: I'm very well and God kept, my life is changing fast. Wife and child to lead about, I'm growing wiser at last. The Lord told me the other day, that your bands had been loosed, And I'm wondering how you're feeling ever since I got that news?

Orion: As you say I'm growing fast as times and seasons go. But do not worry about me friend, this started over ten thousand years ago. I'm still the mighty Orion man and greatly delight in my continual expand. I can still beat all the beasts of earth except for that Scorpius stinging hurt. The Creator designed me to spread and grow, so that my nebulous parts would truly show, that man in all his carnal facts are as unstable as my inner tracks. So you see dear friend so few in years, you need not have so many fears. Just live your life within the Lord, and with His love eternal reward. Enjoy His work and holy ways, keep them in sight while you pray. As night is black and stars are bright we all make an account of our lives.

Norm: Thank you Orion for your encouraging word, a righteous life to be preferred. Goodnight my friend and see you soon, under the light of a big full moon.

Orion: Yes of course I'll see you again and only if it doesn't rain. Goodnight. Norm: Goodnight

Norm

Nothing Empty About This Nest

Our children's independence is a reminder of how much we had to give and all that we have accomplished. It is a pleasure to remember that it is not a form of abandonment but an expression of a job well done.

Madeline Levine

Is it just me, or have the last 8 years just flown by incredibly fast? What is happening to my life that it seems like just yesterday that both of my kids were in high school, and I was running around after them 24/7? Time is a wizard with an invisible wand. Sometimes I wish I could stop the clock and take a look around for a while before it snaps its thieving wand again. I am now an empty nester with 2 college graduates, and their lives are moving at breakneck speed while mine is just trudging along, though somehow I've gotten older overnight.

I need to talk to all these seasoned parent

birds flying around. All these mama birds pushing those babies out to the edges of those nests with their barely wet wings. Does mama have plans to fly somewhere later that day, or is she just picking up the broken shells and hanging new photos over the old baby bird ones? What does she do when she buys too much seed at Costco anyway? Is she okay with all of this? She has to be, right? Because as everyone says, "life goes on."

There is a time for everything, and a season for every activity under heaven. Ecclesiastes 3:1

What a weird feeling it is when life just keeps going on and there is this vacillating feeling of "it feels like only yesterday" to "that was forever ago" when remembering the lives of our children. It's a strange experience to visit the homes of my daughters. It's weird-good, since they are doing so well for themselves, and thriving in good jobs, and actually carrying themselves now. It's bittersweet because as I watch them navigate all the hard things in life, there was once a place in which I inexplicably fit, and now that place is filled by their own growth and independence. My new role is to support, encourage, and be ready to hold those tired wings when they grow weary of flying in the world. This is what we spent years preparing them for-to eventually soar on their own, and to not depend on us for everything, and yet we stand in this odd gap of 'what exactly is our purpose now'? We stand on the edge of the empty nest, knowing we've served our purpose, we've raised them as well as we knew how, but now searching for a new role as parents, and as two individual people who are still as one. **Stand at the crossroads and look; ask for the ancient paths, ask where the good way is, and walk in it, and you will find rest for your souls.** Jeremiah 6:16

We have each gone through our own periods of sadness, missing our girls, and adjusting to two dinner plates instead of four, and having our life shift into a quiet simmer rather than a rolling boil. Children add such a lively energy to a home, and when they leave, it can feel very much like you've lost part of your purpose. But like any change in life, sometimes we need time to stand in it, wear it, accept it, and eventually rejoice in it. There is a bit of grief between each stage of life, as I think back. From the time they said their first word to the time they took their first steps. Every stage leaves something precious behind, but brings with it something new and exciting. If we stay back too long looking at what we're missing, we may not enjoy the excitement and newness going on right in front of us!

We know our daughters still need us, just like we needed our parents when we left home, and still do, though for much different reasons. We are learning to walk the fine line of when to step in and offer our help, and when to hold back. Much like when they learned to walk and we let go for the first time so they could take those first steps alone. We knew they needed to walk on their own in order for their legs to become strong, just like they need to fly on their own in order for their wings to become strong in this world. We are learning where we end and they begin all over again. It's not an easy thing to do, when our whole world of parenting for all those years was centered on guiding and leading them and probably neglecting ourselves a bit. We now have to refocus, because they have a life to live that requires a whole different form of freedom and independence. We have a life to live too, and it starts with remembering how our own life began. We were once two young people, ripe for the world, needing our own independence and identities, and we can't ever forget that as we watch our own adult children grow into who they are apart from us. We would be wise to remember our own identities apart from being their parents as well.

When parent birds are left alone in the nest, they have a choice. They can look up into the sky with pride and enjoy their babies soaring high, as they taught them to do, or they can focus instead on the quiet nest. One will create a new foundation, and the other may create a sense of loss and emptiness. It always gives me comfort to tell the girls they will always have a home here no matter how far away they go. It also gives me peace to look forward to spending time refluffing our own nest, and seeing what new adventures we can create here on our own. It's all in how we choose to look at the changes in life that will determine how well we will adjust to them.

"Fly little bird...your nest will always be here..."

A new foundation can be an opportunity for us to keep on building. I have joked that I may turn the upstairs into a dance/party lounge, but in all seriousness, it's a time to make plans for the future. This marriage started with two and God willing, will end with two. Our children were a blessing, and it went by so fast. We enjoyed so many wonderful times with them, and of course, there are always things we wish we could have done, but we know that of all the kids God could have chosen for us, we got the best two daughters He could have ever created just for us. It's no wonder it went so fast, because good times do that sort of thing. We have sweet memories and so many fun stories to share around the table.

Our grand vision all along was to build a life for them that they would want to share with their own families one day. To have so much love that they would want to build more family memories with the people who loved them their whole lives. We are hopeful for the growth of our family, the additions our nest may see in the future, and for all the changes in our lives to come. There is nothing empty about a nest that is always full of love, hope, and family waiting for you to come home!

Give the ones you love

wings to fly,

roots to come back,

and reasons to stay.

Dalai Lama

Jami

Part three:

Faith

Joy is Contagious....But You Have to Catch it First

Where is your joy? Where do you find it, or rather, who or what supplies it? It's a good question to ask ourselves, and even more important is the answer. Joy is described as a feeling of great pleasure and happiness. Being group-hugged by my family makes me feel incredible joy. Watching my insanely happy, fluffy white dog, Angel come bolting toward me every time she sees me reflects not only her unrelenting joy, but ignites mine as well. I'm not sure there is a finer joy than the sweet smile on a baby's face when you smile at them, but I'm sure we could put our heads together and come up with hundreds of thousands of pure joyful moments. Things that make us happy are the best things! I love to watch people talking about the things that bring them joy. They turn into beacons of light, shining and reflecting on everyone around them. And don't even get me started about people who "smile with their eyes"! They're the best!

That's the great thing about joy. It's contagious, or it should be, anyway. It's also self-generated, to a point, and then passed on to others. When a baby first discovers her toes with her hands, and then brings them to her face for a closer look, what a joy it is to see her face light up with amazement. Secondhand joy can be just as exciting as our own, and sometimes even better. It's when we experience joy bubbling up within ourselves, and then oozing onto others, creating a shared moment of intense glee. When we are happy to see the joy in others-in their love for God, for others, nature, in their accomplishments, their blessings-we will share that same passionate happiness inside too. There is a reason for the saying, "Jumping for joy" because it is a feeling of intense happiness that can barely be contained! I'm not ashamed to say that I can crack myself up, and I'm known for laughing at my own jokes. I can't help it, and I don't even care, but any reason to laugh is good enough reason for me. Laughter is so healing, and such a positive way to spend time with others or by myself, such as it is!

The Bible defines joy much the same way,

except that joy is dependent on who the Lord is, not on who we are, and not on what is happening around us. True joy comes from God, His presence, and living hopefully and confidently in His purpose for our lives, no matter what happens. **The joy of the Lord is my strength.** Nehemiah 8:10 It may be difficult to believe that we could experience joy when there are so many sad and destructive things going on in the world around us, and it may be easier to just blame someone or even God, when bad things happen. Joy is not a feeling based on our circumstances. It is an assurance that the presence of God will be our hope and our peace, no matter the outcome. I sure didn't feel joy when I lost my beloved family members, but I felt the assurance of God's peace as He walked me through those terrible moments, and He is still my peace and comfort where the hurt remains. To me, that is the definition of joy here on earth. The joy in heaven will be the day we are all reunited again. To feel joy is to believe in something better even when everything looks bleak. To radiate joy is to share God's love whether you're at the top of the mountain or at the very bottom of the pit. Sometimes joy looks like happiness, and sometimes it just looks like trust.

We sometimes get so focused on all the things of this world that hurt us, that it can steal the peace right out of our hearts. We steal our own joy sometimes worrying about what we don't have or can't do, or what's happening that we can't control. But when we are relying on God through our hard times, we can trust that He will give us exactly what we need at the right time. **Consider it pure joy, my brothers and sisters, whenever you face trials of many kinds, because you know that the testing of your faith produces perseverance. Let perseverance finish its work so that you may be mature and complete, not lacking anything.** James 1:2-4

There are days I don't feel very helpful, productive, or "happy" by the world's standards, whatever those are. But inside, I know where to find joy, and I can be at peace, when I choose to stay there. I trust what God is doing with me, because I know I have a greater purpose. He's not going to leave me hanging. **For I know the plans I have for you, declares the Lord, plans to prosper**

you and not to harm you, plans to give you hope and a future. Jeremiah 29:11 I may not know what my outcome is going to be, and sometimes I get frustrated with myself, but I don't get frustrated with God. I understand that I may be going through things for the sake of others, and each day I am grateful for what I'm NOT going through. I catch myself in pity-picture mode, and then I tell myself to take a picture of my blessings, because that will last longer!

I remind myself that this world is not all there is, and how I choose to use my struggles will either be for my benefit or my deficit as a person. I find joy in His love for me, and I seek out the many things that bring joy to my heart- my family, nature, animals, music, gardening, laughter, writing, baking, and photography. I look for ways to stir my heart and stimulate my mind, and I believe the Lord helps me with this so I can encourage others to find their joy and passions as well. The Lord has given me hope, and I can give others hope because of Him. **Praise be to the God and Father of our Lord Jesus Christ, the Father of compassion and the God of all comfort,**

who comforts us in all our troubles, so that we can comfort those in any trouble with the comfort we ourselves receive from God. 2Corinthians 3-4

Choose gratitude, and let the joy of the Lord be your strength.

Jami

The Wish

I stood there with my eyes transfixed
under the black of heaven's night
waiting for the streaks of wishing stars,
my heartbeat the speed of light.
I whispered quietly my prayers
as the stars flashed brilliantly,
heart trembling in desperate places,
Would this be my destiny?
For what I asked seemed so unfeasible,
only God could comprehend,
even as the words slipped from me
I was surprised at the "wish" I'd sent.
I waited there, lost in my own world
braced for falling stars to land,
while my answer fell in stardust
and rested in my hands.

Jami

Old Views

It was in the spring of 1993 that I was in Puerto Escondido in the state of Oaxaca, Mexico. We, the graduating class of The School of Ministry, of Kelowna Christian Centre were on the annual international outreach. I was the soul that had been lured into the overseeing position of this motley crew of students. There had been the usual ups and dog day downs when it was revealed that we would be going inland to some very remote churches, in order to minister to the mountain dwellers. Up until this time, we had been evangelising by way of a dramatic play, called The Decision. It had been made for the international audience because its expression was mimed and could easily be grasped by any onlooker regardless of school age. The thought of cooler weather had been alluring to us since it had been a constant humid 1000 degrees, and acting in this heat was very demanding on the students' bodies. The day had arrived and we drove to the farthest destination our trucks could manoeuvre, without causing major damage to them. Pack donkeys had been previously organised to be at this remote location. As the equipment and limited personal gear was being tied and strapped to the beasts of burden, I noticed a sense of adventure arising among the students. Here we were, gringos in the middle of nowhere, speaking the broken limited Spanish that foreign travellers glean in Spanish English dictionaries. I was taking in this scene of light confusion when I became aware of the panoramic vista that stretched before us . The sky was pastel blue and light wisps of stratus clouds that lazily drifted to lands unknown. The trees gave off a shimmering movement that was caused by the heat of the day that was beginning to draw out moisture from the deep canyon plainly laid out before us. The sense was that of a mirage. I became aware that the view had not changed much from the time when the conquistadors had invaded this proud land. The fact that I was seeing and feeling, the same wonder that the soldiers of old had felt, caused me to drink in this moment of time travel. With trepidation they would have wondered what was beyond this valley of great depth and, as strange as it seemed, I could feel their momentary tribulations. My peripheral vision was taking it all in at the speed of light. I could feel in my bones, in a spectrum of time the sensation of being the first European to discover the new world. I was sure that if I listened closely, I would have heard them discussing with each other and their native guides, strategies for crossing over. I noticed a sense of adventure arising among the students. Here we were, gringos. Unlike the explorers of old, I was in the hands of families that had lived here for hundreds of years, guiding us to the established village on the other side of the great expanse. As we walked down the steep, well travelled pathway on the edge of the rust collared rock face, I fell into step with the caravan of local people, students and animals. I continued to ponder on the events that I had just experienced and felt privileged to have stopped and smelled more than the roses. For a split second I had been there in past and present. As we stumbled, tripped, and slipped our way down the rocky surface, we came to a bridge that spanned the river. The local people were washing their clothes and themselves, much the same as they had for thousands of years. Some of the students began to jump, dive and somersault into the deep part of the river. The rest lingered on the river bank absorbing the solace that was prevalent in this time capsule of the past.

We eventually made our way to the village and performed the blessings and duties that were expected of us. We ended up as guests after spending some good quality time with the people. The results of the ministry were very uplifting for all concerned. The day came for us to return, so we packed up the donkeys and went back the way we came. As I reached the spot where I had visualized the past I turned to see it again. A painting of Michelangelo came to mind: God's finger tip is touching man's finger tip bridging the gap between them. I mused in thought and gave licence to my soul to believe that my finger tip had touched the explorers. He was in his century and I was in mine, but we had touched by both being in the same place, leading an expedition to what we felt and believed to be right. How do I know this is so, you say? Well I don't know, except to say, that 500 years ago men came to see what they could on a whim or a dare, and ended up on this same ridge thinking of who had passed there hundreds of years before him. I like to remember that timely appointment in my life when I had the insight that it was possible to reach out and touch the finger of God. May I never stop believing in the possibilities that God is trying to touch me.

Norm

Consistently Consistent

In a defeated tone, I expressed to my friend, "I just wish you'd be consistent with me." I thought what I was asking was simple on my end. Just be the person you were yesterday and all of the days before that! Say what you mean. Mean what you say. Stop being confusing and vague. These conversations became very unsettling to me because I was no longer feeling an even give-and-take in the conversations.

Always curious about exactly what qualities are found in happier people, I put "consistent" on the list. How could consistency lead to a more content life? Why are happier people those who are repeating good habits consistently? I believe they are empowered and not overwhelmed. Succeeding and not seceding. Flourishing and not floundering. Communicating efficiently and not evasively! Consistent people can get things done, and people who are getting things accomplished are people who just seem overall happier with their lives. Are consistent people perfect? Am I always consistent? Of course not, but I am aware that my inconsistencies in certain areas are leading to my unhappiness or dissatisfaction within them. I know that I am unhappy with inconsistent relationships and I am the one who has the power to change them.

If I want to be healthier, I know it's about choosing better foods and eliminating bad eating habits. I can't do it for just one day or even just one week, one month, or even a year. I have to show up every single day and keep repeating the same healthy routine over and over in order to be a strong individual. It has to become who I am and not just what I do. I need to change my behavior, put in the effort, and be consistent.

Some of the quotes I searched on the subject of consistency stated that "Consistency is rare." Is it rare to be consistent or just to experience people who are inconsistent? I don't know that it's rare, per se, but I do think it's challenging at times, depending on the choices we are making. I think the quote I would make about consistency is this- Consistency reveals. It reveals a genuine desire to connect with a person if a relationship is what you want. It reveals a goal, if you are working out at the gym every week and making healthy choices at mealtimes. It reveals commitment, character, priorities, and when being a parent, it reveals patience, or none at all! A lack of consistency reveals something too. What do we want out of our relationships, our friendships, our careers, finances, parenting goals, health, spiritual lives? What we are willing to put our consistent effort and energy into will reveal what is most important to us. If we want something to change, it starts with us, and it's probably going to require us to be consistent.

When thinking about what consistency can reveal, there is an alternate view. When we notice that friend who has not been consistent with us, maybe we shouldn't keep asking them to be a more steady presence for us, but instead just observe. It will reveal to us the truth of the relationship, and we may see our own inconsistencies within them. Perhaps it is better to see others as they are rather than expect actions from them that they are not capable or willing to deliver. Do we really want someone in our lives that doesn't want to be consistent with us? Should we fight to keep people like that around? Maybe we are expecting consistency from the wrong people, and that in and of itself becomes our own inconsistent behavior. My friend was being consistently inconsistent because I allowed it to continue. It's not too much to ask a friend to be loving, kind, or honest with us, but it becomes a problem on our part when we are continually asking it of a person who is not as dedicated to us as we are to them. We need to be consistent too-in understanding that we can't expect others to return to us exactly what we think we have been giving. Sometimes they are not able to deliver because they simply don't care, and we begin to call it inconsistency rather than accept it for what it is.

If we want to accomplish a life in which we are finding ourselves in a more positive state in any area, we need to align our choices with the desired outcomes.If we want to consistently let ourselves down, unfortunately we can do that too, by doing nothing and continuing to repeat that too. I am choosing to invite God into my process by asking Him to help me with the goals in my life that require me to consistently repeat habits that will help me succeed.

Jami

The Partnership

The hypnotic sound of wheels rolling down down, up down the highway. My eyes front focused on nothing in particular, until it catches my eye and even interrupts the sound of the road.

Everything in me is alert to its simple display. I do not know why I appreciate it but appreciate I do. I've come to look at it as a road partner, even a familiar friend that I meet during my work life.

That big bright face causes me to reach for a smile. His ability to have survived decapitation at the mill encourages me to try harder.

Somewhere somehow the Queensland Sunflower let seed fall to grow again and make a lonely roadrunner like me feel a sense of welcome home. Yep! That's why God created sunflowers.

Norm

Drowning

The light in you was life for me
but having missed the fatal, ending cues,
in arid soil of unmet expectations-
I flooded with tears that you refused.
With hope and futile cultivation
watering in vain, thus overflowed
The withered desert of your heart
Hung dark for me, where I once glowed.
In peace, I sprinkled you with forgiveness,
fertile words, though unaware,
Poured over you, sparing hesitation,
Muddied reason without a care.
With every drop in vain, I sought
to ripen sweet on a barren vine,
I saw the light of what could be-
Depleting, consuming, and drowning mine.

Jami

Seasons of Adjustment

Spring promises
Summer maintains
Fall delivers
Winter thinks
Spring promises all that is possible
Summer maintains all that is
Fall delivers what was real
Winter thinks about it again
Spring promises all that is possible and what can be imagined
Summer maintains all that is happening at the moment
Fall delivers what is real and ended up being
Winter thinks about it again and waits for spring.

Norm

We Need The Prayers of Each Other

"When we get to heaven and see who was praying for us and when they were praying for us, we will be both surprised and humbled. None of us are sufficient in ourselves. We need the prayers of each other." Charles Stanley **And when he had taken it, the four living creatures and the twenty-four elders fell down before the Lamb. Each one had a harp and they were holding golden bowls full of incense, which are the prayers of God's people.** Revelation 5:8

Tucked into a bulging old bible of mine are letters from special people, photos, handwritten names, newspaper clippings, and various other paraphernalia, representing people that I have prayed over. Some have left this earth, some are still struggling, and some I don't even know. What a strange realization it is to imagine that they will one day know who was praying for them and when. I have never thought about this until now. I naturally assumed that God would always be the only

One who would know the subject and content of all of our prayers. I know praying for others is important, but when I thought about it this way, it took on a whole different meaning. Our faithful prayers are eternal.

Devote yourselves to prayer, being watchful and thankful. Colossians 4:2 When we pray for another person, whether it is someone we know well or even a complete stranger, it draws us closer to that person. It places them on our minds and in our hearts. It shows we care for them, and it is one way we can show our love for others and our faith in God. It can give us peace, knowing that we are trusting God to help in a situation that we are not equipped to handle on our own. We intercede for others with prayers of healing, protection, salvation, blessings, and any number of requests we may bring to God on another's behalf. It could be someone we see on the street, or a family member that we've been praying for over many years. Prayer is something we should be in the habit of doing continually, and without worrying that it's being done perfectly. I consider it an honor to be asked to pray for someone, and I take it seriously. This is a request I am taking to God, and I'm believing He hears me.

Do not be anxious about anything, but in every situation, by prayer and petition, with thanksgiving, present your requests to God. Philippians 4:6 Sometimes when I am praying for a person, I have no idea what is going on in their lives. I just sense that I am to pray for them, and I do. I may never hear from them or know what is happening, and it's not for me to know. It is a privilege to pray for someone, as it is bringing a person to the Lord and not only asking Him to bless that person, heal them, watch over them, or whatever the prayer may be, but expecting Him to follow through! It is most humbling to pray for someone we consider evil, or an enemy. It's not easy to pray for someone who is hurting you or others, but we are called to do just that.

But I say to you, love your enemies and pray for those who persecute you, so that you may be sons of your Father who is in heaven. Matthew 5:43 I am praying for someone who is no longer actively participating in my life, but as long as God keeps bringing this person to me, I will keep asking God for whatever He puts on my heart for this person. It doesn't matter if you're speaking, on good terms, or if you even know what the person is going through. If a name continually comes to you from God, consider it a request to pray. I don't know what it all means, and I may find out one day, and I may not.

With God, nothing we learn is ever wasted. My prayers for this person may never change them, but they may change me, and while that may sound as trite to you as it does to me, sometimes that is the power of prayer.

When God is in a prayer on either end, there will be a definite answer. I've often heard people say God's answer can be "Yes", "No", or "Wait", but I think another one of God's popular answers seems like silence. He often gives us what we need and not necessarily what we want, and it often feels like silence. It's not waiting. The answer was there all along. We just didn't want to hear it. If our own prayers for others change us for the better, that is an answer. Sometimes in praying for someone else, God will show us where we lacked effort or any number of convictions, if we're paying attention. I have too many examples of how this has played out in my life, but it truly has been the case.

Let us then approach God's throne of grace with confidence, so that we may receive mercy and find grace to help us in our time of need. Hebrews 4:16 When someone tells me they are praying for me or my family, I am very grateful. To take my concerns to the Lord on my behalf says to me that they care, and that they have listened to me. They love and support me and want the best for me and my family. I couldn't ask for more than that. When blessings come my way, and even if the outcome isn't what I expected but I'm still okay, I know it's because those prayers of the faithful are being heard and answered. I am feeling the love behind those prayers and God's peace is resting on me. It's another opportunity to give all the credit and praise to God, and thank them for their willingness to pray.

Therefore confess your sins to each other and pray for each other so that you may be healed. The prayer of a righteous person is powerful and effective. James 5:16 I am praying for you, all who are reading this. I pray that you may have hope and peace, despite the state of this world, knowing that the Lord is, without a doubt, all that you will ever need. May He bless you with the desire to know Him and love Him more, and to greet each day with gratitude and praise. **Be joyful in hope, patient in affliction, faithful in prayer.** Romans 12:12

Jami

Let God Bug You

Proverbs 3:12 For the LORD corrects those he loves, just as a father corrects a child in whom he delights.

In the spring of 1986, I was trying to organize my family's return move to Queensland, Australia. The target date to be in Queensland was mid-July and there were all kinds of things not falling into place for a smooth move back to Australia. A sister in the Lord came up to me and said, "I was praying for you, and I felt the Lord say that if you sold your Cadillac, everything would fall into place, and things would go smoothly." She also remarked that this had been a strong impression in her spirit, even though it seemed an odd instruction. My thoughts were, "I didn't think she is that spiritual and most likely this statement was just her own idea." I wanted to sell the Cadillac in the last week before we left the country so that I had reliable wheels till it was time to leave.

The next day, as I was driving my metallic peacock blue Fleetwood Brougham Cadillac (one of the smoothest driving cars I had ever had to that point) to work, I could feel a nudge starting to bug me, and I speculated that the nudger was God. As I wrestled with the idea of selling the car, my argument kept coming back to the fact that I wanted to sell the car in the last week before we left to return to Australia. However, the nudges became stronger and turned into a conviction that was starting to set in my spirit. By the end of the day, I had unenthusiastically agreed to sell it if a buyer came along. That same evening, I was reading 1Corinthians 6:20 **For ye are bought with a price: therefore glorify God in your body, and in your spirit, which are God's.** I got the strong impression that the Lord was saying I had been bought by Him and everything I owned was His. I then sensed the Lord say that I was not to make a profit on the car because the favour of the Lord was on me and He had blessed me with it at a low price. I was using the car for my business, and because of tax advantages, there was a small loan owing to it. I was to simply hand the car over with the balance due. In other words, whoever got the car was to simply pay off the balance of the loan and the car was theirs.

What God had said was bugging me so much that I blurted out, "If this is of you Lord, then this will take place so fast and will be so clear to anyone involved." Early the next morning, I had to stop by the Bible college where I was teaching a few classes. In the parking lot, a student, Michael, came running up to me and said, "I was praying last night, and asking God for a big solid car that I will need to go to school and work. I need a car that will be able to handle the mileage that I will be putting on it. I heard God's voice in my spirit say to come and ask you!" At that point, I heard an inner voice say, "Is that fast and clear enough for you?" Isaiah 30:21 **And whenever you turn to the right or to the left, your ears will hear this command behind you: "This is the way. Walk in it."** I said to Michael, "Just take over the balance of the loan and you can have the car." His eyes popped and he asked if God had spoken to me. I said, "Yeah, He has been bugging me since yesterday and last night about it." By 11:00 am all paperwork was done and the car was his. The same day, I happened to get an amazing deal from a rental company of which I knew the owner. He offered me a deal that was less than the payments of the loan. The car he had was a big boat of a car that he was having trouble renting because it was so big. The proprietor said I would be able to use the rental up to the day I left for Australia.

The sister in the Lord who spoke that odd instruction, as she had called it, was right. Absolutely everything fell into place in record time. Everything that consists of a move to another country was done, and paperwork was filled out and accepted a whole month before we left. My wife and I had nothing to do except get on the plane and head for Australia. Not only did things fall into place in Canada, but in Queensland, within the first week, my wife and I both had jobs, a furnished house to rent, and a church to attend. Within a short time, we were moving into a house we had bought. We didn't have to do much as God had prepared the way on both continents.

What I realized is that when God is bugging you about something, then let Him bug you until you obey because the stage is being set to bless you. God loves you and is correcting your choices so that you walk towards the destiny He has set in place for you. Proverbs 3:12 **For the LORD corrects those he loves, just as a father corrects a child in whom he delights.** God is not the killjoy Satan says He is. The devil is out to kill, rob, and destroy you, and will bug you to choose sin over life, then when you fall, Satan will kick you when you are down with endless accusations of failure. The contrast could not be clearer. God bugs us with His love to preserve our lives, and Satan bugs us to death to destroy our lives. Not really a hard choice to make here. Let God's love bug you into His kingdom where your life is eternally blessed beyond what you can think or ask. Blessings.

Norm

Little Diamonds

The year was coming to an end in Dec. 82, in the town of Maroochydore, Queensland, Australia. My wife had gone to visit her family in Guatemala and had been gone almost 2 months. I had become very lonely and melancholy as our first anniversary was fast approaching on Dec. 10th., the same year.

I had spent the time preparing sermons that I would minister on Woomby Radio every Monday morning. I was also teaching religious teachings in the high school system on Tuesday mornings. Tuesday nights I helped pastor a church in Maleny and ministered in the Maroochydore assembly on Sundays. Sometimes I helped out in a Christian book store, while at the same time trying to find work in order to live.

The times were hard in Australia at this period in Australian history. Living day to day had become a skill in survival. There were no more holes in my belt to reduce the size in order to keep my britches up.

I wanted to give to my Celeste something special that year and knew it would take a miracle because of the cashless society I was a part of. I was wandering past a jewellery store, when in the twinkling of an eye, I knew the love offering that I would joyfully give to my lover of one year. I brought my request to God, where marriages are made, and let him see the sincerity of my heart, toward his daughter and my wife. "Diamonds are forged in the hottest of fires," God said to my soul, "and it will take the courage of love to bring about this miracle you wish to bestow." As the days passed and time drew near for Celeste to return, I seemed to get broker and poorer and became concerned.

Then God moved His mighty hand and said to me, that Sunday morn."I want everything you have and more and this request of yours will be born."

"I have nothing Lord to give you, I've given all to thee."

"I can see some pennies in a can under the sink. Will you give all to me?"

"Yes Lord. You can have it all, the pennies and can as well, if what you say will be, then truly it will be."

That Sunday morning I gave all to the Lord and after church I was invited to a friend's home for a barbecue. During this time of satisfied eating, a brother came up to me and said, "God has told me to bless you with a gift financially."

The friend said, "I give it in obedience to His majesty for you to do with as you please. God bless you Norm."

The next day I went to the jeweller's store and bought the gift I know she'd adore. They were little diamond earrings so small in size, but paid for with love and a spiritual surprise. I rushed to the airport to find my bride who's gift to me was to arrive. I hugged her tight and hugged some more, thanking God that He had brought her home on our anniversary. What a time we had on our celebrated first. The diamonds were loved with tears, of course, and are still worn today with love and force.

I learned a lot during this trial in God, that when we present our works before Him, the works will be tried with fire. Out of the hottest of flames will come little diamonds for the crown we will give Him. I think I have felt a part of the joy that will be ours on that anniversary date.

Norm

The Lens of Eternity

Eternity is not just the wonderful perfume I wore on my wedding day. I was a romantic young woman who selected that fragrance based on my desire for a marriage that would last "forever." Great marketing for the Calvin Klein company, right? Well, my views on actual eternity have grown a lot since 1994. **He has made everything beautiful in its time. He has also set eternity in the hearts of men; yet they cannot fathom what God has done from beginning to end.** Ecclesiastes 3:11

Eternity as described biblically is infinite time, or a duration of time without beginning or end. It is impossible to imagine what eternity is really like! But it's imperative to know what it means if we are to live a more peaceful existence here.

I have lost many things throughout my life, and I haven't always taken those losses well. Family, friendships, health, and many others. Each time I would lose some type of relationship or opportunity, it would feel like the end of the world. Each time my health would fail me, it felt like every secondary loss that came with it meant my life would change forever. I got tired of feeling the rejection and abandonment feelings that came every time I was let down. I wasn't rolling with the punches anymore. I was just getting battered and bruised all over. **"My grace is sufficient for you, for my power is made perfect in weakness."** 2Corinthians 12:9 What finally changed my perspective was the lens I chose to view my losses through. I was going directly to "doom" thinking. I was taking everything at face value. I was forgetting that this is not all there is. The problems of this world and the hurts in my life are temporary, so I don't need to take it all so hard. Yes, it hurts, but it doesn't need to steal my joy and my happiness with it. Have you ever heard someone say, "We live in the world, but we are not OF this world"? Well, that is what it means to see yourself as an eternal being, and not a worldly one.

Therefore, we do not lose heart. Though outwardly we are wasting away, yet inwardly we are being renewed day by day. For our light and momentary troubles are achieving for us an eternal glory that

far outweighs them all. So we fix our eyes not on what is seen, but on what is unseen. For what is seen is temporary, but what is unseen is eternal. 2Corinthians 4:18

This world is not all there is! And it's not all we are either. That is of great comfort to me, knowing that everything we are going through is temporary, will be used in some way to glorify the God we serve, and we will one day be with God, spiritually new, where none of these worldly problems exist. To be able to look at life eternally is to understand that every small thing that upsets me is basically a waste of time. Every big thing is still big, but when viewed with God's perspective, I don't have to be crushed by it. **Truly, truly, I say to you, whoever hears my word and believes him who sent me has eternal life. He does not come into judgment, but has passed from death to life.** 1John 1:9

When I look at things with an eternal lens, I can appreciate that my health issues are temporary. I will either be healed here on earth or in heaven, but one day I will be restored. The world may be an awful place where terrible things happen, but it's not our forever home if we have accepted Christ as our savior and not the world. When I look at broken relationships from a worldly perspective, there are often a lot of psychological terms tossed around, or confusion about how or who, what or why. But when looked at from God's eternal perspective, it's simple. At least in my experience, forgiveness is the way I can experience happiness in relationships even when they are difficult or non-existent, because I can let go of them and allow God to do the healing. Forgiveness is a gift we give ourselves, not the offender, and it doesn't excuse their offense, only your hold over them and their hold over you. When we let go of grudges and bitterness, we experience peace. When I let go of the world and embrace a heavenly view, I am in a position to love because I am seeing things from God's point of view. C.S. Lewis said, "Everything that is not eternal is worthless in eternity." We can leave behind those things that don't matter here, because they won't mean a hill of beans in heaven anyway, in other words.

Sometimes there are no clear cut ways to put an "eternal bow" on any situation, and maybe we've all struggled with this part of life. Some situations just don't make sense, and it is at these times I have heard people wonder why God would allow such things to occur. As a believing person, I understand their pain, but that is why we have to get to know Christ so that we can walk through some of these really hard times with Him. I've been through many of those, and have all the cracks in my heart to show for it. Each time, my faith has gotten stronger at the cracks, not weaker, even if the outcome wasn't what I had hoped. Trusting God doesn't mean He does what we want. It means we trust Him, and no, it won't always make sense. Thinking eternally means really thinking outside the human box, and that is not easy or even possible for most of us.

And probably the hardest eternal perspective to see was the one I had to find during my periods of grief. One of my most faith-tested times was when I lost my older brother. He was only 50, and taken suddenly and without warning. I was so hurt and so angry, and then I bottled all of those sensitive emotions for a good long time. God heard all kinds of rebuttal from me every day! But

I think back, and I'm guessing He was glad I was still talking to Him. He wants us hot or cold, and never lukewarm. **I know your deeds, that you are neither cold nor hot. I wish you were either one or the other! So, because you are lukewarm-neither hot nor cold-I am about to spit you out of my mouth.** Revelation 3:15-16 All I can say is that through those situations, I have learned to trust God to show it to me at some point, and He will. I have had to learn to give in to His will, because believing in Him and His will for me is so much better than trusting that this world has anything long-lasting for me.

When I lost my dad unexpectedly just 3 years after losing my brother, I wasn't ready to say goodbye, and I still miss his gentle voice and his loving presence every day. But knowing he is waiting for us in the eternal place of heaven is why I can rejoice here on earth. It's why I can be happy when I think of him, and even for my brother, though sad for his sons who are going on without him. I realized that both things can exist. I can be both sad and happy at the same time, and my "world" won't end. I can go on without certain friends, I can go on while certain people think what they want to think. I can go on with health issues doing whatever they're going to do. I can go on while the world rages out of my control. I can because this is not all there is. I never have to feel rejected or abandoned or hopeless for any reason. When God is the first and final stop, there is no loss at all, only the gain of an eternal life with Him.

In my Father's house are many rooms; if it were not so, I would have told you. I am going there to prepare a place for you. And if I go and prepare a place for you, I will come back and take you to be with me that you may also be where I am. You know the way to the place I am going. John 14:2-4

Jami

Part Four:

Thoughts And Notions

Frou Frou Barbecue

This past week has been a real stinker of a challenge. And while I'm keeping the details close to the vest, let's just say "wow, didn't see that coming!" I think it's a pretty good call that I'm in a major testing zone, and someone keeps giving me more tests than I have pencils for! Sometimes life just keeps kicking me right square in the face, but I just keep getting back up. And sometimes I have so much negative going on that I just have to laugh....or I might just lose my mind for good.

I had to make the 3 hour trip to Ann Arbor to see my neurologist today. On the way back we decided to try out a barbecue place, only because my doc was talking about how they had this nitrogen-processed custard we just had to try sometime. He wouldn't stop talking about barbecue and I hadn't had my lunch yet. Sneaky Chuck. So, we were lured into this place mostly by the intoxicating smell that only barbecued foods emit, and we decided to forget our issues for a while and pork out. Pun intended. Side thought, why do places always smell better than the food inside tastes? Looking at you, flame broiled burger places.

We looked over the menu. Turned it over a few times, hoping it had a few extra pages that fell on the floor. Hmmm...This "barbecue" seemed a little "weird", I thought. I started peeking at hubs over my giant menu kind of funny. I mean, this guy knows his barbecue. He's the best griller, smoker, and meat flipper in our family, so I already know this place has no chance with me at all. But I examined all the menu items several times, and there was nothing basic to be found. No pulled pork sandwich. No smoked chicken. No brisket. Nothing a regular barbecue place would have at all. I'm reading things like *topped with arugula*, *deep fried pickles*,*chipotle mayo*, *goat cheese topping*, *radishes*, and some *weird freaky aioli*, and on and on. I gave him my *this is a secret conversation* look, and he leaned in close to hear me say, "This is frou frou barbecue".

Yep. It's much like the last barbecue place we visited in a big city area. It's jumping with loud music, I mean, really loud, but it's stuff you don't recognize if you're over 40, because it's somewhere on the satellite channel of "frou frou barbecue on the 2's". And yeah, it had the weird Nitrogen ice cream/custard thing, but it tasted like that icy cheap stuff we bought at Aldi that we left in the freezer too long with the lid off. I mean, I'm not against loud or new music, but someone was awfully depressed, crying for their mommy, and another was screaming, and I couldn't find the beat at all. None of the sandwiches seemed to come with just regular ole buns, and they didn't have regular soda. Not even a Coke! Just a bunch of strange-sounding concoctions that may or may not have contained basil, sea salt, and lavender.

After seeing all of the strange and scary smoky things they put in poor old basic macaroni and cheese, and the smoked croutons in the Caesar salad, I lost it. I mean, I'll try new things, I'm not a big baby, but come on, they messed with barbecue. BARBECUE. Who does that? Stop trying to put pine nuts and sharp-edged lettuce on my brisket. Pine nuts? I don't want lime basil soda and screaming sad people on the radio. Who are you? What is happening? STOP IT! But I just sat there with that strange look on my face instead.

I wanted to plead with the guy with the plaid skinny pants, " Go to Kroger and just get me a bun. On a plate. Put some smoked meat on the bun. Put a bun on top of the meat. Bring me the plate. No sweet potato fry. Real potato fry. And a Coca Cola! No frou frou." But instead, we ordered soup. Mexican SOUP. At a barbecue place! And it felt weird.

We ate that Mexican soup and that Italian bread that came with it, and that really strange icy and not creamy ice cream, tipped our sweet server finely, and we high-tailed our 40 and 50 -something butts out of there. Obviously we were not frou frou enough for that barbecue place at all. We turned up our classic rock music we know all the words to (the music you grew your hair out for), and enjoyed the ride home.

There really is no place like home for the best, true true barbecue and an ice cold Coke. Sometimes keeping it real is best. Live and learn, I guess. Live and learn.

Jami

No Answers Please

????????????????????

Will the years speak kindly of me? Said my soul in thought or will I have lost the race of remembrance that I gainfully sought?

What can I leave here or in heaven above that will be known as kind? What will be regarded as uniquely special? Well you know... "truly mine?"

Will good treatment of wife and young really count? Or that we had granted through stewardship ample amounts.

Can I attain greatness by activities done? Or shall I have bitterly lived a life undone?

Will my inner man always mock the conscience I own, with accusations and slanders that demand painful groans?

Who will know in the eternal system that I had been, a man of vision often held back by the turmoil within?

Gratis I have grace and abundant life this be true. However, do I come across as a person to you?

Am I of value in the events of time? Or

dare I ask these queries that revolve in my mind?

What if these questions I ask were known?
I may not like the answers of this twilight zone.

Norm

Tikal

The clear rustling sound that came from the undergrowth and the dead foliage that covered the jungle floor, was unsettling to the primal fears that lurk in the deep subconscious of my mind. Phil, Leonardo, and I, were walking toward the rented jeep, when a tarantula the size of a large man's hand went scurrying to our right at a very rapid pace. Moving faster toward us, the spider darted over and under fallen palm leaves, moving these obstacles at will. Increasingly our insecurities grew, but as this prehistoric hunter rapidly changed directions, our nervousness eased. "Hokie-Dina, did you see the size of that thing?" Phil said. The relief was evident in his voice.

"It kind of makes the hair on your neck stand up doesn't it," I said, with equal relief that the tarantula had moved on to stalk something more its size. "This has been some kind of day," I said, as the bravery of my downtown Anglo-Saxon courage came back to me. Smiling in amusement, we reflected on the day's events and discoveries.

The morning had started off in the back streets parallel the airport runway, in Guatemala City. Looking at length for signs of life in the misty early dawn, we found the obscure airflight office of the Tikaljet Company. Checking in was easy. If you had the money, you were on the next flight. Drowsily sitting there, I overheard numerous tourists complaining about the service they had been receiving since their arrival. Irritated by their conduct, I became more embarrassed, when I heard them say that they were from Canada. What do they want, a drive up window to a Tim Hortons, twenty feet outside the waiting room door? Phil seemed to notice their verbal intrusion into his exotic, Latin, and lost in time experience. Sitting down across from me, he pulled the visor of his baseball cap down to cover his eyes. For Phil, this action seemed to make these aliens with no manners disappear. If it can work for him, I thought, I'll do the same, while praying for their insipid discontented souls.

Flying over Guatemala City as the sun rises, presents a spectacular scene. Known as, "The Land of The Eternal Spring Season,"

Guatemala is in floral bloom all year long.

Displaying the multiple colours of green, the land beneath us disappeared as we found our altitude and speed above the clouds. Our destination was The Ruins of Tikal. For years, I had wanted to photograph the Mayan Ruins that have perplexed historians for centuries. Divine appointment seemed to be on my side.

Landing instructions were communicated by the Spanish flight attendant, as we arrived in good spirits.

"Welcome to Flores!" said the Rent-a-jeep clerk with a perfect smile. "Our jeeps can go anywhere in the state of Peten, and satisfaction is guaranteed."

Leonardo looked at me and said, "Oh! Oh!" Quickly and forcefully, Leonardo's bartering skills acquired us a small jeep that had us on our way. Thirty eight miles from the airport, and some distance on a dirt road that followed the shoreline of a pristine lake, we found a wonderful hotel called Camino Real.

Loading up the cameras with black and white film, we headed out to the Maya Ruins that were another forty miles north of our location. We meandered our way through the national park, on roads that curved in and through a lush green tropical canopy of jungle. The morning heat was rich in warmth, and soothed the aches and pains that had made their residence in my bones, through the Canadian winter. I felt my soul, spirit, and body thaw as relaxation took over my complete being. Finally, arriving at our destination we three amigos parked the jeep and moved toward the paths that were ancient highways, of a people that had established this area in 700 B.C. Hundreds of birds, of all kinds squawked and screamed their songs, as they displayed the vast variety of colour that embroidered their beauty. As we walked and came upon the first of the many ruins, exclamation of amazement boomed from our mouths."Ah la," said one.

"Incredible," said another. "Hokie-Dina" came the last.

Look at what I found! was repeated over and over. This seemed to be the effect these ominous giants had on us. It did not matter that thousands of people had seen and discovered these ruins before us. We were convinced that we had discovered them, and could not shake this feeling all day, regardless of the amount of other people we met, in this old city, from a lost world. We allowed our imagination licence to run wild as we walked on the rock hard surface of the ancient architecture; exploring under them and through secret passageways in them. "Click, click, click," the shutter-release captured moments from a historic past that could be seen and heard as the sounds of old echos bounced from these solid icons. We made our way to the area known as the Great Plaza, when in the zenith of its history, was once home to one hundred thousand people. Climbing the numerous steps of the forty seven metre high pyramid known as The Giant Jaguar, we took in the spectacular view of the entire city of old. While drinking in the vista that Tikal offered, a loud and clear yelling sound came from Phil as he stood on the top of the temple, pointing at a large toucan bird, with its characteristic fluorescent colours across its large beak, flying two feet over Phil's head. "Look! It's Toucan Sam" he shouted. "It's Froot-Loops. Hey it's Toucan Sam. Did you see it? Hey! See it?"

Leonardo and I were laughing heartily at the scene, and so were the people from all over the plaza, as they looked up at Phil.

"Woops,"Phil said. I guess that was a pretty gringo thing to do, huh?"

Carefully stepping down the eighty odd thin steps, we entered an area that was recessed into a large stone wall and found a maniacal looking mask, taller than we were made of solid stone. Next to the mask, we found an entrance to a newly discovered cave, and entered it. This was a doorway to another civilisation, that was five hundred years older than the ruins on top. With a small flashlight, we groped our way through the cool, claustrophobic, and blackened passageway. The light beam spied out different angles and cracks in the cavern walls. Suddenly, we were face to face with a large three foot square carving of a serpent's head, that jutted out from the wall to intimidate and remind the cave dwellers of old, who it was they served. "Look at that," said one.

"Spooky",said another.

"Hokie-Dina" said Phil. This is the best and weirdest discipleship training I've ever been on. Finding our way back to the light, we were hit with the intense heat of the unforgiving jungle. Finding a shady spot, we drank deeply of some cool refreshments, and then decided to climb some of the higher temples, farther up the pathway.

Years of gnarled root growth had claimed the base of the Bicephalic Serpent Temple that stood about 65 metres high. Hand over hand, and step by step, we made our way to the top lip of the temple. A solid steel ladder had been affixed to the wall, and allowed us to climb to the very pinnacle of the temple, which offered a view of incredible magnitude. A full three hundred and sixty degree view above the thick rich green canopy, was ours to photograph and enjoy, with complete amazement. The haze caused by the heat of the day hung on the horizon, as we could see for miles and miles. The tops of the different temples shot through the treetops, appearing as guardians of these ancient forests. Looking down on this picture of the past and present, I became aware that I had fulfilled one of my life goals and I was not disappointed with the results.

Rustling sounds brought us back to the present, and the memory of the tarantula with the nine inch wide body, somewhere behind us. "Let's move on," Leonardo said, as we peeked over our shoulders.

"Yah! a good idea," I agreed.

That night, as we ate in the dining room on the open balcony, overlooking the emerald coloured lake, the sun burned off the rest of its light, as it set below this old and prehistoric land. The satisfaction of a goal achieved was apparent, and I allowed the good feeling to wash over me, as I rested in the warmth of the evening tropical breezes.

The rest of our time was filled with kayaking, eating wonderful delicacies, and good healthy fun. I had shot off countless rolls of film and had taken plenty of time to rest and contemplate the future. Phil and I entered into all sorts of theological discussion with much enthusiasm, and deliberated on the purpose of ourselves and mankind.

As we left the humidity in this corner of the world on a twelve seater, twin engine prop plane, we looked down to see the vast, intricate landscape, and I hoped I would see it again, sometime soon. The small aircraft, with its loud drone, fought the thermal winds and air pockets, which caused us to be bounced about like a cork on a rough ocean. Like characters in a 1930 movie adventure story, we hung onto what we could, and endured the flight back to Guatemala City. Free falling, between thunder heads, the run-way drew near. "What are we doing tomorrow?" Phil said,

"A photo shoot of a Spanish sixteenth century city, called Antigua," I replied.

"Hokie-Dina, I've never had discipleship training like this!" In reflection, I responded, "Well, discipleship is an adventure." "Yah, it sure is," Phil said, as we landed.

Norm

Look And See

I saw a man a short distance off
Who had baggy pants with stitches across
With worn out shoes upon his feet,
A belt of hemp, he walked the street.
I saw a dark lady walking so fine
With rhythm of movement she felt inclined
To move her head from top to side
And sing her music being made inside.
I saw a pensioner making his way
With a bright colored shirt and his hair all gray
I could see by the grin that marred his face
His cheque had come in with one day's grace.
I saw myself in a new polished mirror
And what was revealed relieved all fears
That no matter how old I seemed to grow
My life in control, Christ did show.
Amen.

Norm

Masked

Masks I wear are many, hiding awful thoughts.

A mask that fades the odious me that others peeringly saw.

A mask to hide my appetite of lude and shameful ways.

I hide my real self very well from many looking on, their idea of me.

I come out as polished bronze.

I lie. I cheat.

I stimulate the masks that cover me, that no one knows.

The frightened breath breathes inside of me.

My hope is that one day in life these masks will tumble down.

But did I write this to mask the thought that I might be found?

There is One who knows me true. He created me long ago.

No mask I use can stop the burn of His judgmental stare and glow.

Figleaf to smiles, I've tried them all, but none

seem too fair.

His love to me is real, you see, and it keeps me standing bare.

Norm

Still Water

If my words could reach where my thoughts wander
a tumbleweed of script would touch the paper,
and deeper still would move with wonder
the souls of those who grace my heart.
If I could say what I would say if only I could speak
heart burning on my sleeve, hand stretched out to reach,
pent up waves would crash- revealing
warm and blue, and dreams of seasons
gentle strength, abandoned reason
eyes searching, weighted by lack
Spilling truths for those who listen.

Jami

Chastised

My father chastised me because I was
My mother chastised me because of my
father
My teacher chastised me because I thought
My wife chastises me because I do not think
My son chastises me because he is learning
how
My life chastises me because I fight it
My Lord chastises me because He loves me
My chastisement is real.

Norm

The Fire

Captured by flames, my eyes entranced,
crickets serenade for one last dance.
Good night, warm summer evening, good night.
Stars twinkle out their cosmic names, some I will remember,
glowing above the swaying pines, the moon is but a sliver.
The caress of pine enchantment carries my mind to reminisce,
smoke swirling through my hair,
Knees hugged tight into my chest.
Dancing sparks, I feel your friendship.
Passion as the torch of blue,
twirling flames of love as one,
Your abiding fire - truth.
Ashen heaps of desolation,
disregard and lamentations-
once brightly blazed, now lost in mournful

endings.
The fleeting promise of fitful embers-
smoldering, coaxing, glaring red,
their final farewell - luminous and tender,
breathing life back into the dead.
Steady my heart, while memories creep
like smoke that spirals thick and deep.
And wistful yearnings grow to be
the hopeful flame that sighs in me.
Goodbye sweet summer nights, goodbye.

Jami

When You're Smiling

It was in the spring of 81 in Katoomba, New South Wales, Australia, that my fiancé and I had gone out to embrace an evening of joyful escape. I was in Bible school at the time and Celeste was a preschool teacher's helper. We often gave patronage to interesting cafés and restaurants that lined the historic, windy, steep hilled streets of Katoomba. On this fresh windy night, we had gone to a Greek Italian hangout that offered savoury foods that were pungently marinated in garlic. All the food served had delightful surprises for the pallet, but nothing attacked the taste buds like the garlic bread. Its strength was legendary, as often it would be remarked 3 days after eating it, someone would say 'were you at the Greek's place today because I can smell garlic..?'

We feasted on a variety of foods that the menu had seduced us to fall into. We drank of each other's thoughts as we peered over the rims of steaming coffee cups, our eyes speaking volumes to each other. Our free hands would seek out each other's fingertips around the collage of spent dinnerware and basket of garlic bread. Oh! How this created a natural smile from the heart. If this moment could be bottled and greedily sucked when needed, there would be no need of marriage counsellors. We always think this way when first in love, because lovers are such givers. As it became time to leave this paradise of time out from the everyday, we made our way down the street arm in arm whispering love notes and being full of ourselves. The sidewalk was busy with other people shuffling their way through, and to, life's appointments. Then a man who had earlier been alleviated of some of his shyness by indulging in his favourite libation began to sing and sway to the tune of "When you're smiling, when you're smiling, the whole world smiles with you.." This intermission in our walk brought such a laughter to our souls that we hummed a few bars with the gent and continued to do so as I walked my future bride to her home.

I have not forgotten the truth of that night and often think of this strange messenger of good cheer. I hope he is as happy as he made us feel that night. So remember, "When you're smiling the whole world smiles with you."

Norm

Chopsticks Francaise

Feeling the hot sun burning its solar colour into my body was about the only thing happening on the beach this tropical day. I had been musing on the one month South Pacific tour I had been travelling on and reflecting upon the clean fun I had experienced. I would be returning to Canada in a few days and I had begun to think of work and other preparations that would have to be fulfilled upon my return.

Noticing a shadow blocking out the sun's rays, I looked up as I heard a young man say. "Hey man! Does anyone want to go out on a catamaran for a few hours? Only five bucks each." A couple of people who had been sun worshipping on my left and an intimate couple on my right said they would go. With not much to do, I figured I would do the same.

We cast off on a triple pontoon catamaran that was of fair size and beauty. Tightly woven nets had been affixed from the centre pontoon to one of the outer ones creating a webbed floor which allowed a person to lay down and watch the water fly by underneath one's body and sometimes feel the cool splash of salted sea water that would spray and refresh ones brown coloured skin.

The captain's first and only mate boarded at the same time we were scrambling aboard. She was carrying containers of take-out Chinese food which she stowed away in a type of food storehouse valise. We sailed out directly toward open seas. Lapping waters could be heard caressing the hull as we sailed into deeper waters in search of sea turtles. Standing on one of the pontoons holding on to some rigging, I looked back and the clear view of Diamond Head's peak reaching toward the heavens on Hawaii's coast could be appreciated for its size and magnitude. Peacock blue water and celestial blue skies were medicinal to the soul and body as we clipped along at a fair pace. Arriving at a shallow area in the middle of nowhere, the captain asked if we wanted to go swimming, so he tied up the sail and dropped the anchor in the shallows. Diving and snorkelling with sea turtles that glided underneath the catamaran was truly majestic. The clearness of the water was magnificent as the seafloor could be seen to be about twenty feet below. After a short swim we headed onward drying off in the warm breeze created by the swiftmoving craft that simply glided atop the ocean.

After sailing for some distance and time, the Asian first mate took the Chinese food and offered some to the different passengers that were lazily enjoying the ride. Hearing her speak with a French accent, I asked her in French, where she was from. "Vietnam," she said as she separated the take-out into a plate while handing me a pair of chopsticks at the same time. Accepting the food and sticks, I confessed to her that I did not know how to use chopsticks. "Viens içi, je vais te montrer comment," she said with a sincere smile. Sitting next to her on a small folding deck bench we put our plates on the top of the food valise and lesson one was on its way. As the instructions were given, immediate progress was evident as food made its way to my mouth, and in a short time I was proficient with the sticks. At this moment in time a pure sense of irony was upon me as I thought of what was now happening. I, a Canadian, was being taught the art of using chopsticks by a Vietnamese first-mate who spoke to me in French while we ate Chinese food on a catamaran made in California, off the coast of Hawaii. The moment had a certain international flavour about it, and I was loving it. Right now this moment in time belonged to me.

Hugging the coastline, we continued sailing the catamaran and enjoying the salt scented breeze that bathed us in tropical warmth. I asked the first-mate about the life she had left in Vietnam. She described in a censured manner the horrors that had been experienced by her and her immediate family, as a result of the war. She went on to say that life was getting better and was grateful to have escaped Vietnam. I supposed that sailing a catamaran on the coast of Hawaii could not wash away all her nightmares, but could probably lighten the load of them and lessen the frequency of their visits as time went by.

It never ceases to amaze me, in that everyone has a story. We are all from somewhere and have been through some of life's difficult events. Some people go through much worse trials than others- but nonetheless, we all have an individual story that makes us who we are. Truly we are all human beings that breathe air, drink water, and need food to live. We grow up with needs,wants, and desires that define and shape our characters, thus in turn affecting our destiny.

It comes down to the fact that we are all in need of each other because we are first human, then a nationality. The need for each other may vary from person to person but nonetheless, there is a fundamental need to be known and to know who and why we are. I am a human being first and a Canadian second.

All too quickly the beach came into view and my sailing adventure came to an end. Thanking the captain and first-mate for a most unforgettable time, I said "good bye, and bon jours, merci beaucoup." In my heart I was thanking them for giving me a living moment when I felt good about my humanity. I walked up the beach and realised that I never got to know the first-mate's name. Strange, I thought, as I pondered what she had taught me that afternoon while drifting on the Pacific. Yes! On this day March 13th, 1979, I had learnt to use chopsticks, but more so, I had learnt to see the good side of human character.

I looked back and could see the brightly

coloured sails bob and cruise outward. I got that Lone Ranger feeling, so I smiled as I said. "Who was that masked woman?"

Norm

We hope you have enjoyed our thoughts. We also hope that this book might encourage you to write your thoughts down and see what the Lord has been teaching you over the length of your lifetime. Blessings and peace be on us all.

About The Authors

Proverbs 18:24b But there is a friend who stays closer than a brother.

Thoughts For A Friend is a collection of poems, short stories, and commentary that were put together by Jami Lynch Rogers and Norm Sawyer, who met through their blogs. By divine blessing, they became fans of each other's writings, and through their love for the Lord, they developed a friendship that has held up to God's scrutiny. Jami and Norm hope the thoughts and words in this book will encourage and bless your heart.

Connect

Jami Lynch Rogers Blog jastrogers.blogspot.com

Norm Sawyer's Blog www.sirnorm.com

www.ingramcontent.com/pod-product-compliance
Lightning Source LLC
La Vergne TN
LVHW020719110826
845149LV00012B/2328